Knowing the Truth about Education

OTHER TITLES BY THE AUTHOR

Reality and Education: A New Direction for Educational Policy (2013)

Knowing the Truth about Education

Daniel Wentland

ROWMAN & LITTLEFIELD
Lanham • Boulder • New York • London

Published by Rowman & Littlefield
A wholly owned subsidiary of The Rowman & Littlefield Publishing Group, Inc.
4501 Forbes Boulevard, Suite 200, Lanham, Maryland 20706
www.rowman.com

Unit A, Whitacre Mews, 26-34 Stannary Street, London SE11 4AB

Copyright © 2015 by Daniel Wentland

All rights reserved. No part of this book may be reproduced in any form or by any electronic or mechanical means, including information storage and retrieval systems, without written permission from the publisher, except by a reviewer who may quote passages in a review.

British Library Cataloguing in Publication Information Available

Library of Congress Cataloging-in-Publication Data

Wentland, Daniel M.
 Knowing the truth about education / Daniel Wentland.
  pages cm
 Includes index.
 ISBN 978-1-4758-2018-8 (cloth : alk. paper) — ISBN 978-1-4758-2019-5 (pbk. : alk. paper) — ISBN 978-1-4758-2020-1 (electronic) 1. Educational change—United States. 2. Educational planning—United States. I. Title.
 LA217.2.W46 2015
 370.116—dc23
                                                                    2015013058

∞™ The paper used in this publication meets the minimum requirements of American National Standard for Information Sciences—Permanence of Paper for Printed Library Materials, ANSI/NISO Z39.48-1992.

Printed in the United States of America

Contents

Preface		vii
Acknowledgments		ix
Introduction		xi
1	The Useless versus the Useful Politician	1
2	Education Is Not the Input/Output Model of Business	11
3	Yes, There Is a Right and Wrong	19
4	The Wrong Paradigm: Traditional Schools versus Charter Schools	31
5	Lacking a Love for Learning	45
6	Students Are Part of the Problem	49
7	Bad Teachers	53
8	The Myth about Maximizing Student Learning	61

9	A Disconnection in the Educational Pipeline	71
10	Getting Education Right Isn't Rocket Science, but Many Make It That Way	77

Preface

The advancement of knowledge and the development of new skills and abilities are the keys to success in today's technologically advanced society. For education to fulfill its role, educational programs, practices, and policies must be based upon reality, not educational myths and political ideologies. We must understand that the same old way of thinking and the same old way of doing things will result in the same old educational outcomes. To improve education, we must be willing to open our eyes and focus upon educational realities, not the latest fads in teaching, or the "hottest" curriculum suggestions or political ideologies.

Given the reality of budgetary restraints, a pivotal issue confronting educational leaders is how to establish strategies that maximize dollars spent while increasing the effectiveness of the learning environment. The information in this book clearly outlines the obstacles that interfere with and cause confusion over what needs to be done in order to improve the educational process. Effective educational policies can only be constructed and implemented if we are willing to move away from the myths associated with education and push aside political philosophies.

If you can handle the truth regarding education, then please read on.

Acknowledgments

First, I want to express my appreciation to the readers. I look forward to your comments; please contact me at daniel@danielwentland.com.

Next, a big thanks to Dr. Thomas F. Koerner at Rowman & Littlefield for giving me another opportunity with R&L.

Thanks to my editor, Dr. Andrew Kelly.

Finally, my days are always brighter with Kathy, Dakota, Scarlett, and Hailey.

Introduction

The following statements reflect fundamental principles that impact educational outcomes:

- **The Mission of Education.** A formal educational situation should provide an exceptional learning environment that prepares students for meaningful personal lives, professional accomplishments, and responsible national and global citizenship. In sum, the purpose of formal education is to maximize the learning environment—period. Political ideologies and social agendas must be put aside so the true mission of education can be focused upon.
- **Learning First.** Simply put, the learning environment must be the focus of the decision-making process. Improving the knowledge, skills, and abilities of students and teachers must be the top priority. This is the foundation of a student and teacher–centered approach.
- **Community of Learners.** Quality teaching and research are the foundation of the learning process. Everyone engaged in the formal educational process should place value on intellectual and personal achievements, accept diversity of thought, engage in professional development, and support service to the community. The concept of lifelong learning must be embraced.
- **Academic Excellence and Accountability.** In the pursuit of excellence, educational programs should offer challenging curricula, utilize effective teaching and learning methodologies, consist of a

research component, and demonstrate transparency and intelligent accountability.
- **Personal Responsibility.** The educational process should instill in each individual a sense of acceptance and responsibility for the outcomes of his or her personal decisions and actions.
- **Motivation.** "There is nothing better that motivates people to make the investment of time, energy, and commitment than to grow better at something that has importance. Failure may be the initial motivator, but it is increased competence that leads us to do more and more" (Fullan, 2007). Motivation is about establishing an environment where individuals have the opportunity to grow better every day.
- **Collegiality and Respect.** The educational community should acknowledge and support the rights of others to express their beliefs and viewpoints, and their right to disagree within the framework of civility. Each individual should feel a special connection as a valued member within an academic organization.
- **Leadership.** An effective administrator strives for excellence, creates a collaborative environment, and develops the full potential of all members within an organization. Knowledge of the fundamental principles of management, organizational behavior, marketing, educational leadership, and economics is an asset when examining the issues confronting educational leaders and decision makers.

Taken in their entirety, these fundamental principles regarding education, learning and motivation, leadership, and teaching excellence provide a starting point for grasping how to increase the effectiveness of the educational system. When a system is working right we marvel at its effectiveness and like any system, the educational system can become more effective if we focus upon the realities of the learning environment; nothing short of that will get education right.

Given the goal of getting education right, our course of action becomes straightforward. We must delve deeper into the realities associated with learning and the obstacles blocking the educational system from functioning effectively. Only after completely unmasking the true nature of the educational process can we hope to fully understand what the educational system can actually accomplish. That's the truth, hard as it is to accept.

As we move ahead in our quest to uncover the truths regarding the educational system, the information in this book is laid out like a road map leading us to our final destination of getting education right. More specifically, each chapter is built upon an educational reality or educational obstacle, and in the end, a clear picture will emerge of what needs to be done to get education on track.

CRITICAL POINTS TO REMEMBER

The truth is often hard to face, but if educators and politicians continue to avoid the realities associated with the educational process, then enormous amounts of time and energy will continue to be spent chasing a variety of educational illusions.

Simply put, chasing educational mirages ultimately leads to nowhere.

The information in this book moves the educational process off the nowhere track and onto the reality track where the educational system can become an effective mechanism for improving learning.

The question now becomes: Who can handle the truth regarding the educational process? Which educators, politicians, students, and members of the public have the courage and open-mindedness to see reality?

REFERENCES

Fullan, M. (2007). *Leading in a culture of change* (rev. ed.). San Francisco: Jossey-Bass.

1

The Useless versus the Useful Politician

Being able to handle the truth regarding education begins with the realization that the relationship between political ideology and educational policy is one that needs to be severed. To understand why, let's learn more about the useless politician. To begin that effort, let's start with a quote from Larry Millett's book, *Sherlock Holmes and the Red Demon*. In that book, Sherlock Holmes is asked, "Now, Mr. Holmes, what will you need to begin your investigation?" Holmes replied, "The facts. They are the foundation of all that will follow."

In the never-ending quest to improve educational performance, educators and politicians chase after the most recent technological breakthroughs or the latest learning techniques or the "hottest" trends in leadership or curriculum theory, much as puppies race in circles trying to catch their tails. After all that frantic scrambling around, what emerges from those misguided efforts is, at best, a short-term spike in some student performance numbers. Long-term educational solutions remain a mystery.

The learning process will never be maximized while we continue to search for silver-bullet solutions and allow politicians to keep forcing their political agendas upon the educational system. Injecting political ideology into the educational environment is the first characteristic of a useless politician. The useless politician does not care about outcomes, but instead is primarily motivated by the desire to expand his or her political power and advance a political ideology to achieve the societal goals embedded within it.

> ## AN EDUCATIONAL REALITY
>
> Steady, long-term educational results require more than chasing fads and being guided by educational myths and political ideologies.

The useless politician talks a lot about equality and the importance of outcomes but never examines what outcomes are being achieved. All the useless politician focuses on are the intentions of his or her policies, not the actual outcomes. To the useless politician, the outcomes are generally ignored or, worse, lied about, because the outcomes for the most part don't support the intentions. The useless politician lives in the world of false intentions, never in the world of reality and cold, hard facts, because the facts shatter the illusionary intentions.

> ## THE USELESS POLITICIAN
>
> The useless politician lives in the world of false intentions, never in the world of reality and cold, hard facts because the facts shatter the illusionary intentions.

Because the useless politician is so fully indoctrinated in his or her political ideology and blinded by the glittery intentions of the ideology, the useless politician never freely admits that he or she has made a mistake or that the political philosophy and policies are imperfect. On the rare occasions when the useless politician is forced to admit that a mistake has occurred, the mistake is minimized, and the admission is usually communicated in such a way that the situation remains in a state of murkiness so that blame can be easily passed around. As the blame game heats up, the true nature of the mistake and subsequent outcomes can be hidden under layer upon layer of confusion and deception.

In fact, the useless politician thrives on deception and acts like a magician using sleight-of-hand tricks of communication and other actions to cover up the facts or divert attention away from the outcomes of a policy or political ideology. By the way, major policy blunders are never fully acknowledged by a useless politician because to accept the fact that a major mistake has occurred would threaten the foundation of the political ideology that fostered the mistake. Above all, in the eyes, heart, and mind of a useless politician, political ideology must never be questioned.

> **THE USELESS POLITICIAN**
>
> The useless politician is an artful dodger, and above all else, his or her political ideology must never be questioned.

Another characteristic of a useless politician is the tendency to attack successful and productive individuals, because successful and productive individuals do not need useless politicians. Useless politicians need individuals who are dependent upon the policies and actions of the useless politician, for this creates a false sense of the importance of the politician and the governmental policies established by the politician.

The message and political actions of the useless politician are focused on convincing individuals that the main, if not only, reason that they are not successful is because of the individuals who are successful and productive. Let's be clear: being productive, not dependency on the government, is the key to increasing the probability of a successful life. The useless politician creates dependency for the most part.

What does it mean to be productive? Being productive means that an individual has valuable knowledge, skills, and/or abilities. Life demands that each individual make a decision as to whether he or she wants to be productive or not. Individuals who decide to be productive increase the probability of living a more successful life than individuals who decide to be mediocre or worse; a truly great society fosters the notion of being productive, not dependent. But being productive is not the message the useless politician wants individuals to hear.

To put it simply, productivity is the foundation for economic growth. Individuals and societies that are productive have a higher standard of living than unproductive individuals and societies. Does anyone want to leave a productive society to live in an unproductive society? If we are honest, the answer is no. To be more specific, who would rather live in North Korea rather than the United States or Canada or Germany or any democratic country? Is any rational person willing to risk his life to enter North Korea or other countries led by a totalitarian government? Totalitarian governments are characterized by limited personal opportunities, shortages, and minimal productivity levels.

Productivity, scarcity, incentives, decision making and choices, and opportunity costs are fundamental concepts rooted in the economic way of thinking, which represents the logical flow of ideas that form the basis for the academic discipline of economics. All economists are initially taught to utilize the economic way of thinking to understand the world; however, it's funny, but sad, that many economists eventually lose their focus and begin to support political policies that violate the fundamental principles upon which economics is based. The lure of best intentions pulls some economists away from the reality of outcomes, and soon they become no better than the useless politician.

To the useless politician, the economic way of thinking represents a threat to their political views because the economic way of thinking focuses on the independence of an individual, not dependency. Remember, the useless politician is primarily concerned with status, and his or her status grows with dependency, not productive, independent citizens. Thus, success and being productive must be attacked by the useless politician. How often do you hear a useless politician blame successful individuals for the lack of success of others? The attack on success is part of the artful dodge of the useless politician, for that attack diverts attention away from the policies of the useless politician that are the root cause of many of the social problems that exist today.

Personal accountability for decisions, not blaming others for one's own failures, hard work, limited and effective government, and striving for excellence are values that help people lead a meaningful life. Dependency on the policies, programs, and actions of useless politicians and centralized governmental initiatives are the pathway to nowhere. Paraphrasing one of the many statements of Jesus, "You can give a man a fish and he will eat for a day, but teach a man to fish and he can eat for a lifetime." The useless politician is only interested in giving a man a fish so that the man will always need the useless politician; the situation becomes a matter of survival for the man.

> ## THE USELESS POLITICIAN
>
> The useless politician promotes dependency on government, not being productive.

The best way to help individuals become successful and lead meaningful lives is through a complete understanding of the economic way of thinking, for that economic framework encapsulates the real world, not some utopia.

The first economic reality of the world is the notion of scarcity, the idea that wants outstrip the factors of production, which means decisions must be made. We cannot have everything that we want, thus decisions become an important aspect of life. From a societal perspective, every society has had to come to grips with three economics questions. The first question is what to produce. The next question is how to produce the goods and services. Finally, the third question deals with a distribution idea: Who receives what has been produced?

Linked with decision making are the economic realizations of opportunity costs and the impact of incentives upon the decision-making process. An opportunity cost reflects the economic reality that with every decision, something has to be given up or sacrificed. In other words, to get more of something, something else must be reduced; getting more of "A" results in less of "B." In addition, a decision will be influenced by incentives; if a positive incentive is put forth, an individual will respond in a positive manner, and a negative incentive will invoke a negative response. Policy makers must always be aware of the incentives of a policy. The key question involving policy making should be whether the policy will make a person more productive, or less. Only policies that make an individual more productive should be instituted.

Given scarcity and the need to make decisions and the consequences of the decisions, we return to the fundamental economic, personal, and societal decision of whether an individual chooses to be productive and live a meaningful life, or take the path of being mediocre and living a less successful and, in most situations, a less fulfilling life.

The useless politician conveys a message that if one's life is less successful it is because of successful individuals, or the various organizations or institutions within the society, or frankly, anything else associated with the society other than the choices that the individual has made. This deceitful ploy by the useless politician is quite successful and fosters the notion of dependency and entitlement, and for the most part, results in twisting the economic way of thinking and leading a productive, meaningful life inside out.

The policies, practices, and actions of the useless politician develop a "victim mentality" that permeates every corner of the society, destroying the notion of personal accountability, just like cancer erodes a once healthy body. It is a sad cycle of poverty and despair that the useless politician creates for many in society, but the useless politician can always point the finger at some other source.

THE USELESS POLITICIAN

The bottom line is there is no place in a society
for a useless politician and his or her policies and programs.

Given all the individual and social problems that the useless politician creates, how can we spot one and, as the political slogan goes, "vote the bum out of office"? The answer is rather straightforward. First, do not be deceived by the manner in which the useless politician presents himself or herself, because the useless politician specializes in putting on a good show; everything they say will sound good.

Once we put the show aside, focus on the policy statements and ask one question: does that policy provide an incentive to be productive? If the answer is no, you have uncovered a useless policy, and if the politician generally advocates policies that do not support being productive, you have unmasked a useless politician. We can call this the Milton Friedman test, for he always tried to get the point across that it is the outcome of a policy that is important, not the intentions.

> ### SOCIAL POLICY
>
> One of the great mistakes is to judge policies and programs
> by their intentions rather than their results.
> —Milton Friedman

Now that we have described the useless politician, what does all that have to do with education? Frankly, it boils down to what the useless politician values above anything else, and that is his or her status and power. The useless politician is always trying to control everything in society, and as mentioned, the results are usually mediocre at best.

To the useless politician, education, like every other facet of life, must be controlled from the top down. The curriculum and academic programs must be in tune with the ideology of the useless politician, which is a philosophy that promotes the blame game, us against them, and the "victim mentality." This unhealthy trinity of the blame game, dividing individuals against each other, and creating a "victim mentality" seeps into the educational environment as the useless politician blames teachers and the school system for academic failures. Personal accountability of the student has little or no place in the educational policies and practices of the useless politician.

Once again the useless politician is the master illusionist and opens the door to policies that appear to have merit, but in reality only foster mediocre performance outcomes. But that's par for the course with useless politicians, creating useless outcomes. There is a big difference between

> ### THE USELESS POLITICIAN
>
> The bottom line is there is no place in education
> for a useless politician and his or her policies and programs.

accountability and intelligent accountability; unfortunately, the useless politician rarely is involved with intelligent accountability. Thus, if education is truly going to be improved, the first step must be to overcome the useless politician.

Given the useless array of educational policies that a useless politician will develop and force upon the educational system, how can we identify the useless politician? Once again, the Milton Friedman test can provide a guide. If the educational policy does not focus upon educational realities and promote individual responsibility and a personal commitment to becoming productive, then the policy is useless. (See my book, *Reality and Education: A New Direction for Educational Policy* for a detailed explanation of the realities of education.) If the majority of the policies that a politician advocates are not based upon educational realities and do not encourage personal responsibility and an individual desire to strive for excellence, then that politician is a useless politician. Useless politicians hinder educational progress. Education is about learning, not solving an array of societal problems that have been primarily caused by the policies of the useless politician.

The useless politician versus the useful politician.

Given the characteristics of the useless politician, how can we describe a useful politician? Basically, the useful politician is the polar opposite of the useless politician. Useful politicians understand the economic way of thinking and support public policies that encourage self-reliance and personal accountability by encouraging individuals to be productive.

The useful politician understands that fostering dependency upon government programs has nothing to do with being compassionate or helping the poor. Dependency is about achieving political power and placing the politician above the rest of society. The useful politician promotes independence from the government and supports policies that promote individual and societal productivity, for that's the path that leads to achieving a satisfying life. In short, the useful politician focuses upon the realities of life in terms of setting social and educational policies.

> ## THE USEFUL POLITICIAN
>
> The useful politician is the polar opposite of the useless politician.

Given the useless versus the useful politician, who is the individual that would better serve society as well as the educational community? The answer is quite obvious, thus the real question is: Why would anyone support useless politicians?

CRITICAL POINTS TO REMEMBER

- The economic way of thinking is the fundamental framework for understanding the world in which we live. Those who ignore this truth, including many economists, will always do more societal harm than good. Policy intentions do not matter; it's the outcomes that count.
- The ingredients for a successful life include: personal accountability, hard work, limited and effective government, and productivity instead of, not government dependency.
- The first step to improve education is to overcome the useless politician. That's the truth, hard as it is to accept.

REFERENCES

Friedman, M. (December 7, 1975). Interview with Richard Heffner on *The Open Mind*.
Millett, L. (1996). *Sherlock Holmes and the Red Demon*. New York: Viking.

2

Education Is Not the Input/Output Model of Business

Handling the truth regarding education means accepting the fact that the production of goods in the business world and the development of students in the educational field are not the same thing. A reality check is necessary to understand why.

The traditional model of business is illustrated by a systematic gathering of the elements of production (land, labor, capital) and combining them with an effective production process to produce an output (a tangible product or service). Underlying the entire process is the emphasis upon efficiency and quality so that the product is manufactured at minimal cost and satisfies the expectations of the purchaser.

Given the input/output model, why does one organization appeal to consumers while others struggle to attract customers even though both are operating in the same industry? How can organizational performance be outstanding one year and average or worse the following year? Why does a company with a quality product fail in the marketplace? Why are so many individuals disappointed with their work environment? What drives productivity and value creation? What distinguishes a great place to work from an ordinary or miserable one? What determines organizational performance? How can some of the largest global organizations such as Bank of America, Sears, Citigroup, J. C. Penney, and McDonald's perform so poorly after being such colossal leaders in their industry?

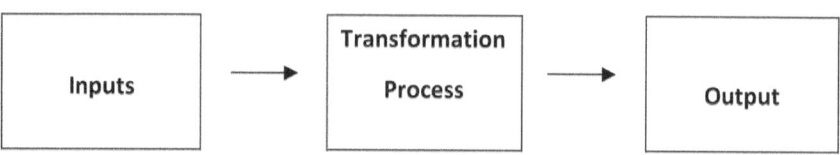

Figure 2.1. The Input/Output Model of Business

All these questions represent a small sample of the critical topics that management and leadership experts grapple with in their quest to understand the forces that impact organizational performance. In 1961, Harold Koontz, author of *The Management Theory Jungle*, summarized the various research approaches that have evolved to address organizational, managerial, and leadership issues. Koontz divided these investigative approaches into six "schools" of thought.

- The first category of scholarship is known as the management process school. Fathered by Henri Fayol, this school of thought examines the functions of management (planning, organizing and staffing, leading, and controlling) in an attempt to improve the management process.
- The empirical school of thought analyzes "real-world" cases in the hope of determining what works and what does not in certain situations. Ernest Dale's comparative approach would be an example of this line of inquiry.
- The human behavior school studies how the behavior of individuals impacts organizational outcomes. The premise of this school is that the study of management should focus upon interpersonal relationships since managing involves working with people in order to accomplish certain tasks and organizational goals.
- The social system school utilizes system theory to understand group and organizational performance. Major contributors to this school include Chester Barnard and Herbert Simon.
- The decision theory school can be characterized by its concentration on the decision-making process and the belief that the development of management theory should primarily focus upon analyzing and improving that process.
- The mathematical school views management as a field of study that can be evaluated and improved through the use of mathematical models.

The problem with viewing organizational performance through a particular school of thought is that the analysis becomes too compartmental, or as stated by organizational behavior researcher, Gareth Morgan, "a way of seeing is a way of not seeing." With such a narrow research perspective what has been lacking is the development of a "macro" or comprehensive approach that combines various elements from each school of thought. It's sort of like trying to piece together a jigsaw puzzle without seeing the entire picture of the puzzle on the front of the box. Without the benefit of seeing the whole picture, the task of fitting together the pieces of the puzzle becomes more difficult. By analyzing organizational performance through a comprehensive framework, a complete picture can emerge that more fully addresses the many unresolved questions relating to organizational success or failure.

From a macro or comprehensive perspective three primary factors impact organizational survival: (1) the internal environment of an organization, (2) the external environment, and (3) the element of chance that can tilt an organization toward success or failure.

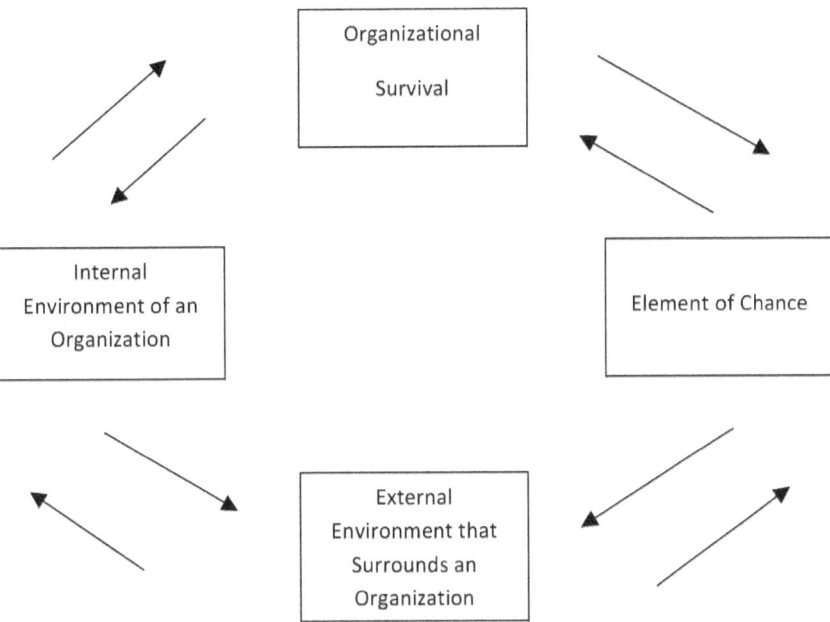

Figure 2.2.

Organizational survival depends upon activities that create an internal environment geared toward achieving a high level of productivity while continually scanning the external environment for conditions that may be favorable to the organization in an attempt to reduce the probability that survival will solely hinge upon the element of chance.

At this point, given our focus on organizational survival, it might be a good time to take a moment to consider a more basic question, what exactly is an organization? Broadly, the term *organization* refers to a group of people working together to attain common goals. Researchers have tried to understand the nature of an organization by utilizing a variety of descriptions and analytical approaches, a summary of which is contained in my previous books, *Strategic Training: Putting Employees First, Organizational Performance a Nutshell*, and *Is Your Organization a Great Workplace?*

For this book, we can simply state that from the body of research devoted to studying organizational development, three common elements have been cited to describe an organization: (1) people, (2) a goal or purpose, and (3) a structure (meaning any phenomenon created by the members of an organization) that defines roles and positions and processes and limits the behavior of members of an organization. Put simply, without people, a goal or purpose, and some form of structure, there is no organization! Of the three elements of an organization, *people* constitute the most important factor, because without human beings, the other two elements cease to exist.

THREE ELEMENTS OF AN ORGANIZATION

People
A Goal or Purpose
A Structure

Once the three elements of an organization are brought together and an organization is formed, a culture develops. To gain an insight into the dynamics of the culture of an organization, we must now think of an organization as a system consisting of a group of interrelated or interacting elements forming a unified whole that works toward a common goal by accepting inputs and producing outputs in an organized transformation process.

A dynamic system essentially has three basic interacting components or functions: an input function that involves capturing and assembling elements that enter the system to be processed; a processing element or transformation process that converts an input into an output; and the output that has been produced. A cybernetic system includes two additional components: feedback and control. *Feedback* is the data about the performance of a system. *Control* involves monitoring and evaluating feedback to determine whether or not a system is moving toward the achievement of its goal(s).

In addition, a system can either be classified as an open system or an adaptive system. An *open system* is a system that interacts with other systems in its environment. An *adaptive system* has the ability to change itself or its environment in order to survive.

Every organization has all three components: input, processing, and output. An effective and efficient organization has all five system components working together as a harmonious whole while having the capacity to interact with other systems and successfully adapt to changes in the marketplace.

If your organization is underperforming, it is the systems that have been established within the organization that are producing those poor results. Unsuccessful organizations are dysfunctional systems. To correct the situation, those systems must be either modified or abandoned (in which case new systems will need to be developed).

AN ORGANIZATION, CULTURE, AND A SYSTEM

An organization is a system influenced by the culture of an organization.

A system is a group of interrelated or interacting elements forming a unified whole that works toward a common goal.

Poorly designed systems produce poor outcomes.

So with an understanding of organizational culture and systems theory we have come full circle by expanding the basic input/output model of business into a cybernetic model that must be adaptable if the system is to survive. However, what is missing so far is the connection between the input/output model of business and the role that the model can play in education. In other words, why can't business system information apply to education? The straightforward answer is most of it can't, and with that answer we are forced to face reality. The realization of reality is hard to accept. Being able to handle the truth regarding education requires facing reality, accepting it, and designing policies based upon reality.

REALITY AND THE INPUT/OUTPUT MODEL OF BUSINESS AND ITS ROLE IN EDUCATION?

The realization of reality is hard to accept.

The basic input/output or expanded cybernetic model of business, for the most part, cannot be applied to education.

Given reality, why do so many politicians, educators, business executives, and the public at large continue to push policies based on the myth that educational process can be modeled upon the input/output model of business?

First of all, it seems that many individuals do not want to face reality, whether it's the reality associated with business, economics, or their personal lives. For those who wish to dismiss reality, let's be clear: reality does exist, but a complete explanation of that statement is for another book. For now, let's continue with the realities of education.

So why can't educators and others, such as politicians, apply the input/output model of business to education? First of all, in the world of business, many of the inputs (raw materials) are standardized. If my product is making a cardboard box, the raw materials (paper, glue, and so forth) will be consistent. If my company wants to make a high-quality box, then the paper and other raw materials will be of a higher quality, but standardized. Each box will be constructed from the same amount of raw materials. If my company wants to produce cheaper boxes, the quality of the paper and other raw material will be less, but once again, standardized throughout the production process.

The ability to standardize raw materials does not apply in education because the raw materials are the students. Are students standardized? I believe we will agree that the answer is no. Thus, the reality that students are quite different from each other dismisses the input/output of business as a valid educational model. Reality is a hard thing to get around, when you are willing to face it.

REALITY IS A HARD THING TO GET AROUND, WHEN YOU ARE WILLING TO FACE IT.

Students are not standardized, thus the input/output model of business cannot be applied in education.

For those who still cannot face reality, let's think about the transformation process of the input/output model of business. The production process in business focuses upon standardization, which promotes specialization and drives productivity, which results in lower costs. When making a cardboard box, the entire production process will be standardized so that each box will have the same dimensions and quality level. Any breakdowns along the production process are corrected so that the standardization of the product is maintained.

Total Quality Management (TQM) principles as well as other management techniques are centered upon specialization and the standardization

---

THE MANUFACTURING PROCESS

The manufacturing process is the physical process of transforming inputs into outputs.

The manufacturing process in uniquely capable of producing standardized products.

of the production process. In fact, the nature of the manufacturing process, including raw materials, labor tasks, and machinery, is uniquely capable of producing products with as little variation as humanly possible.

Can the educational process be standardized like the manufacturing process? I think we can agree that the answer is probably no. Further, do we want the educational process to be just like a manufacturing process? Again, if we are willing to face and accept reality, there will always be some deviation to the educational process. Not all students will come out as the same product. Once again, the truth is hard to accept.

CRITICAL POINTS TO REMEMBER

- Manufacturing inputs (raw materials) are standardized; educational inputs (students) are not standardized.
- The manufacturing process is standardized; the educational process is not standardized. However, the real question should be, if the educational process can be designed to mirror the manufacturing process, is that what we want?
- Since the educational process is not the same as the manufacturing process; not all students will come out as the same product.
- Being able to handle the truth regarding education requires facing reality, accepting it, and designing policies based upon reality.

REFERENCES

Koontz, H. (December 1961). The management theory jungle. *Journal of the Academy of Management* 4(3), 174–88.

Morgan, G. (1997). *Images of an organization* (2nd ed.). Thousand Oaks, CA: Sage Publications.

Wentland, D. (2007). *Strategic training of employees: Putting employees first.* Amherst, MA: HRD Press.

Wentland, D. (2009). *Organizational performance in a nutshell.* Charlotte, NC: IAP Press.

Wentland, D. (2014). *Is your organization a great workplace?* Charlotte, NC: IAP Press.

3

Yes, There Is a Right and Wrong

Facing the truth regarding education means understanding that the teaching of traditional values must be an integral part of any school curriculum. However, before focusing upon values and the school environment, let's journey into the realm of unmasking who we really are.

> There's one problem with all psychological knowledge—nobody can apply it to themselves. People can be incredibly astute about the shortcomings of their friends, spouses, and children. But they have no insight into themselves at all. . . . When people turn their psychological insight-apparatus on themselves . . . the brain hangs. The thought process goes and goes, but it doesn't get anywhere. It must be something like that, because we know that people can think about themselves indefinitely. Some people think of little else. Yet people never seem to change as a result of their intensive introspection. They never understand themselves better. It's very rare to find genuine self-knowledge. It's almost as if you need someone else to tell you who you are, or to hold up the mirror for you. . . . You have to start seeing things as they really are, and not as you want them to be." (Crichton, 2002, pp. 77–78)

To see reality requires a thorough internal analysis that can lead us to an understanding of our behavior. Behavior is based on people's perception of a situation, their personalities, environmental factors including culture and life experiences, their attitudes and motivational influences, all combined together like ingredients in a recipe being mixed together to form a particular dish. It is the differences in perception, personality, environmental factors, attitudes, and motivation that make each person unique and account for our individual differences and behaviors. In fact, the term "individual differences" refers to the notion that people differ in a variety of ways.

WE ARE DIFFERENT FROM EACH OTHER BECAUSE OF

Perception
Personality
Environmental Factors
Attitudes
Motivation

As we live out our daily lives, every minute we spend on this planet defines who we are, why we behave the way we do, and how we react to other people. Ultimately, the behavior of all individuals is a function of their perception of the environment that surrounds them, their personality, their attitudes, and their motivational influences.

An interesting peek into the behavior of the first president of the United States was illustrated in an exhibition entitled *Treasures from Mount Vernon: George Washington Revealed* at The New York Historical Society building in New York City. While wandering around the numerous displays of documents, clothing, pictures, furniture, and a miniature model of Mount Vernon, I stumbled upon a letter written by an individual who wrote the following: "I have attended many occasions at Mount Vernon and have noticed that Mr. Washington rarely speaks and when he does it is never about himself," a revealing comment about the inner being of one person from the observations of another.

Unmasking our inner being, the self beneath the shell of our body, involves an analysis of perception, personality, attitudes and motivational influences.

Perception is the selection and organization of environmental stimuli to provide meaningful experiences for the perceiver. Perception involves searching for, obtaining, and processing information. Perception repre-

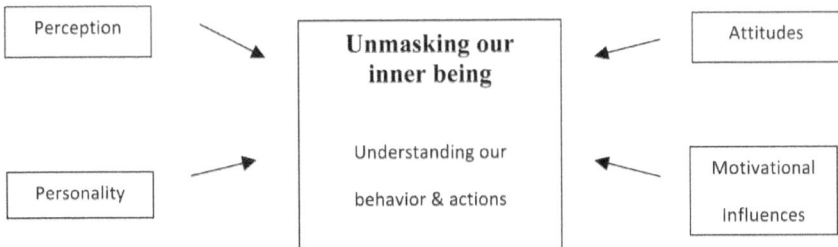

Figure 3.1.

sents the psychological process whereby people take information from the environment and make sense of their worlds.

How we perceive our environment is influenced by internal and external factors. Internal perception factors include attitudes, motives, interests, personality, learning experiences, cultural background, and expectations. All of these factors are aspects of the person (or perceiver)—the individual looking at a target and attempting to interpret what he or she

Table 3.1.

External Perception Factors (Characteristics in the Target)

Size—the larger the size, the more likely the factor will be perceived.

Intensity—the more intense (bright lights, loud noises, intensity of writing), the more likely the factor will be perceived.

Background (Contrast)—factors that stand out against a background or that are not what people expect are more likely to be perceived.

Motion—a moving factor is more likely to be perceived.

Repetition—a repeated factor is more likely to be perceived.

Novelty or Familiarity—either a familiar or a novel factor in an environment attracts attention, depending on the circumstances.

Proximity—objects that are close to each other will tend to be perceived together rather than separately. As a result of physical or time proximity, we often put together objects or events that are unrelated.

External Perception Factors (Characteristics of the Situation)

Time—the time of day can influence what might be perceived.

Work setting—a particular situation, under a particular set of circumstances, in a particular work setting might increase the chances of being noticed and influence our perception.

Social setting—a particular situation, under a particular set of circumstances, in a particular social setting might increase the chances of being noticed and influence our perception.

sees. External factors are characteristics that influence whether the stimuli will be noticed. For our purposes "the stimuli" can be referred to as any environmental event that may produce a response in an organism. External perception factors include: characteristics in the target, what is being observed, and the situation-characteristics in the immediate environment that influence our perception.

To illustrate the importance of perception, let's consider a thought experiment that Albert Einstein utilized when developing the theories of special and general relativity. The thought experiment grappled with the question of whether two individuals would see two bolts of lightning (traveling at an identical speed and distance) strike two poles at the same time if one of the individuals was in a moving train while the other was standing halfway between the two poles? Both individuals would be holding a specially designed mirror that would allow each of them to continually see the lightning as well as the two poles.

Given this setup, the experiment provided a theoretical methodology for evaluating whether two individuals witnessing the same event would see the same thing. Using common sense, we probably would predict that the two individuals would see the lightning bolts strike the poles at the same time since each of the bolts of lightning would be traveling at the same speed and distance toward the poles. Unfortunately, that evaluation would lead us to an incorrect conclusion because the individual positioned in the moving train would first see the lightning strike the pole in the direction that the train was heading and then witness the other pole being struck. The person standing half way between the two poles would see the lightning bolts strike the poles at the same time.

For us, the story illustrates the notion of perception and how two individuals observing the same situation (environment) may not see the same thing, and that creates a problem when we are trying to objectively examine our inner being and the environment in which we live.

The bending and twisting of reality that perception can create stems from two sources. The first source relates to the internal and external perception factors that were previously outlined. The second source (referred to as the *self-serving bias*) focuses upon our tendency as human beings to attribute our successes to internal factors while placing the blame for failures on external factors.

In other words, when we succeed at something our perception is that the success was achieved primarily because of our efforts, while at the other end of the spectrum, our failures and disappointments are perceived as occurring because of outside forces not under our control. The self-serving bias allows us to mentally "pass the buck" regarding our actions and provides a convenient outlet for not taking responsibility for our decisions, which when left unchecked can easily lead to a complete divorce from what had actually transpired. This separation from reality forms an effective barrier to honest and sincere self-analysis, an analysis that must occur because we need to understand who we are and how our behavior and actions influence the performance outcomes that can be achieved.

Given the illusionary barriers that can be erected as a result of an individual's perception, how can the veil of misperception be pulled back so that we can objectively see who we are and how we influence the environment around us? No easy answer exists, but an examination of the attribution process can provide some guidance. According to organizational behavior researchers, Hellriegel, Slocum, and Woodman (1983):

> The attribution process refers to the ways in which people come to understand the causes of others' (and their own) behaviors. Attributions play an important role in the process of person perception. Attributions made about the reasons for someone's behavior may affect judgments about that individual's fundamental characteristics or traits (what he or she is "really like").
>
> The attributions that employees and managers make concerning the causes of behavior are important in understanding behavior in organizations. For example, managers who attribute poor performance directly to their subordinates tend to behave more punitively than managers who attribute poor performance to circumstances beyond their subordinates' control. A manager who believes that an employee failed to perform a task correctly because she lacked proper training might be understanding and give the employee better instructions or training. The same manager might be quite angry if he believes that a subordinate made mistakes simply because the subordinate did not try very hard.

In the end, the relationship between attributions and an individual's perception of success or failure is linked to four causal factors: ability, effort, task difficulty, and luck. Causal attributions of ability and effort are

Table 3.2.

Internal Attributions
I succeeded (or failed) because I had the skills to do the job (or because I did not have the skills to do the job). Such statements are ability attributions.
I succeeded (or failed) because I worked hard (or because I did not work hard). Such statements are effort attributions.
External Attributions
I succeeded (or failed) because it was easy (or because it was too hard). Such statements are attributions about task difficulty.
I succeeded (or failed) because I was lucky (or unlucky). Such statements are attributions about luck or the circumstances surrounding the task.

internal (under the direct control of the individual) while causal attributions of task difficulty and luck are external (not under the direct control of the individual).

The four causal factors of success or failure not only play a pivotal role in analyzing and dissecting how an individual's perception of a situation might blur reality but more importantly, the four causal factors of success or failure provide an individual with a mechanism for gaining some insight into his or her behavior and actions. The more an individual understands his or her behavior and actions, the further that individual can walk down the path that leads him or her toward unmasking who he or she really is.

Perception can cloud our judgment, skew our notion of reality, and warp our understanding of who we really are. To burrow beneath the flesh and bones that form our physical image we have to take an objective look into our spirit. As the misunderstood hero in the movie *Shrek* stated to his

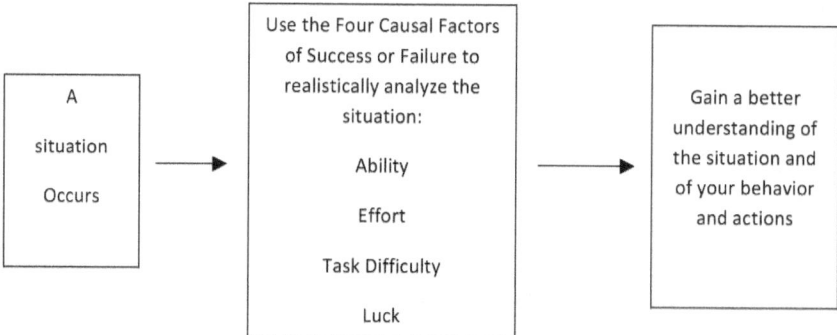

Figure 3.2.

donkey companion during their journey to rescue the princess, "An ogre has many layers," and it's time for us to peel back the layers that cover up our personality—the core of our being.

Personality can be referred to as consistency in behavior and how we react to events and situations. Debate continues regarding the degree to which our personality is determined by nature (heredity and genetics) or environmental factors such as culture, family, group membership, and life experiences (nurture).

In addition to these two factors, a third dimension of personality focuses upon the interplay between the situation and the individual. Although one's personality tends to be stable and consistent, under different situations a particular aspect of an individual's personality can dominate the behavior of a person. For example, a nonviolent individual placed in a life-threatening situation will probably become quite violent in order to survive. These three dimensions of personality (heredity, nurture, and the situation) form a complex web that drives our behavior and provides important clues to examining our inner being—the true entity that exists within the walls of our flesh.

Stemming from the three dimensions of personality, like flowers blossoming on the vine, are the various theories that attempt to explain our behavior. These theories create a pool of information that increases the body of knowledge regarding personality—an intellectual expansion that ultimately moves us closer to understanding ourselves. The theories

Table 3.3.

Descriptive Theories

Type theories classify people into a certain personality type (Type A and B personalities, Myers-Briggs Type Indicator, and Internalizers-Externalizers).

Trait theories look at enduring characteristics or tendencies that describe an individual's behavior (Sixteen Primary Traits, The "Big Five" Personality Factors).

Developmental Theories

Psychoanalytic theories of personality development tend to portray human motivation as self-interested and uncivilized unless socially acceptable roles and outlets are provided.

Humanistic theories assume that human nature is essentially positive, productive, and growth oriented, and that people would develop in healthy ways if they knew how.

Learning theories apply basic principles of learning to the development and function of personality.

of personality can generally be divided along two broad "schools of thought"—descriptive theories of personality versus developmental theories of personality.

What can generally be gained from the theories of personality is threefold. First, personality theory offers a framework for evaluating the extent to which a person believes that he or she is a worthwhile and deserving individual (self-esteem), and second, based on a person's self-esteem an individual's actions and behaviors can be better understood. Third, embedded in an individual's personality is the rigidity of that person's beliefs and his or her openness to other viewpoints (dogmatism).

Environmental factors that influence behavior revolve around the cultural environment that an individual is exposed to. Think of a cultural environment as a kaleidoscope of societal elements that swirl around absorbing and influencing every individual caught within its grasp—like the twisting winds of a tornado scooping up everything in its path. Specifically, a cultural environment consists of the attitudes and perspectives shared by a group of individuals, meaning that a unique society has been formed.

Besides being molded by the societal fingers of the culture in which we live, the events of daily life also leave a unique mark upon who we are and how we behave. In fact, the combination of culture and life experiences such as our family environment, the location(s) where we grew up, the schools we attended, the work situations we encountered, our love relationships and the friends we have chosen are probably responsible for approximately 50 percent of our personality.

For some individuals the experiences of daily life have left them bitter and viewing the world as a hostile, empty, and foreboding place, while for others the opposite is true. What's important for us to remember is that each of us must be aware of our power to positively or negatively impact the outlook of another person. Stopping to offer a few dollars to a homeless person trying to gather enough money to have a meal at McDonald's or helping out at a charitable event may not alter the overall circumstances of a person who's struggling to survive the harshness of poverty, disease, and homelessness, but the fact that an individual is willing to help a less fortunate person speaks a great deal about that individual. Being able to look beyond ourselves no matter what circumstances we have encountered in life is a critical quality.

So far in our quest to unmask our "true" essence, we have explored perception and personality—including the environmental factors that surround us and impact our decisions and behavior. Flowing from our perceptions and personality are the attitudes or opinions we have adopted. We express our opinions about everything ranging from a particular coaching decision during a football game to what we think about another person to the quality or worth of a piece of art. Our opinions or attitudes may or may not be based upon any facts but the attitudes and opinions we have adopted bring us a step closer toward revealing our inner being, our soul, if you like.

At the end of the movie *High Plains Drifter*, the leader of a notorious band of outlaws is frantically looking from side to side in the hope of spotting a fast-shooting, mysterious drifter, and he shouts in a desperate, haunting tone, "Who are you?" As sweat drips down the face of the outlaw and fear fills his eyes, the only response from the drifter is a bullet that ends the outlaw's life upon this Earth. Hell is the next stop for the outlaw, and quite possibly for the mysterious drifter, too.

Fortunately for us, in our quest of self-discovery most of us have not had to engage in a violent struggle between the forces of good and evil, and the middle ground between those two extremes, but we have had to wrestle with the concepts of perception, personality, and attitudes. It's the mixing together of those concepts that molds us into who we are—just like a sculptor chisels upon a piece of marble until the desired form is achieved. The end result for the sculptor is a work of art. The final outcome for an individual is the development of a particular approach to life. Every human being tends to view life from one of two perspectives. These two perspectives or approaches to life not only define who we truly are but also guide our actions and behavior.

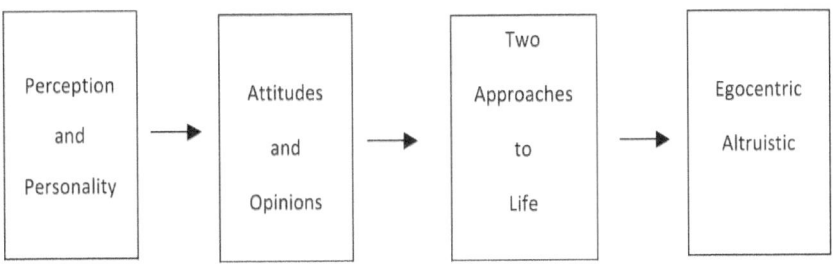

Figure 3.3. Understanding Who We Are

An egocentric person is primarily consumed with satisfying his or her needs. In other words, an egocentric individual is self-centered, adopts a Machiavellian philosophy, and in the end, is only concerned with what is best for him or her; nothing else matters. An altruistic person is a rational decision maker, weighing benefits versus costs while being guided by a code of ethics. The altruistic person has a deep concern for the welfare of others. In other words, an altruistic person can look beyond his or her interests and needs.

> An egocentric person is focused on him- or herself.

For an altruistic person, moral standards are important, and shouldn't our schools be actively engaged in promoting an altruistic approach to life? If so, then ethics must be a critical part of a school's curriculum. Yes, there is a right and wrong, and a person learns that by studying ethics. There is no place for moral relativism in our schools. A viewpoint of "Well, that depends on the situation," fosters an egocentric perspective to life.

> An altruistic person is focused on others.

If you are willing to accept this truth and deal with reality, then what values should be promoted in our schools? The Ten Commandments and the Golden Rule are a great beginning, and then add personal accountability, striving for excellence in all aspects of one's life, and being open-minded to various viewpoints. If the educational system promoted these principles, what a better society we would live in.

To clarify, I am not suggesting that a particular religion (or the Ten Commandments with religious overtones) be implemented within the educational system, just the ethical standards embodied within the majority of the commandments. What is wrong with actively advocating the following?

- Honor your father and your mother.
- You shall not murder.
- You shall not commit adultery.
- You shall not steal.
- You shall not bear false witness against your neighbor.
- You shall not covet.

Now add:

- Take personal accountability for your decisions.
- Strive for excellence, and do not settle for being mediocre.
- Be willing to accept other ideas and practices.
- Treat others as you want to be treated.

School curriculums based upon these values set the stage for better student, faculty, and school performance and build the foundation for a caring and productive society.

CRITICAL POINTS TO REMEMBER

- Developing an ethical code of conduct lies at the heart of an altruistic approach to life.
- A person who develops an altruistic approach to life will make society better.
- Schools should incorporate the values of the Ten Commandments and the Golden Rule into the curriculum, and actively develop individuals who adopt an altruistic approach to life. Personal accountability, striving for excellence, and promoting open-mindedness must be virtues that are promoted throughout the educational system.
- Being able to handle the truth regarding education involves acknowledging that there is a right and wrong; there is no place for moral relativism in schools.

REFERENCES

Crichton, M. (2002). *Prey*. New York: Harper Collins.
Daley, R., and Eastwood, C. (1973). *High plains drifter* [film]. Carmel-by-the Sea, CA: The Malpaso Company and Universal Studios.
Hellriegel, D., Slocum, J., and Woodman, R. (1983). *Organizational behavior* (7th ed.). Minneapolis/St. Paul, MN: West Publishing Company.

4

The Wrong Paradigm
Traditional Schools versus Charter Schools

> To understand the school choice movement, we must understand economics.

Beneath the stars lies our everyday world, a world seemingly far removed from the forces that guide the universe, a world apparently not concerned with the time and space aspects of the cosmos, but instead focused upon the economic forces that play a major role in shaping the lifestyle of every human being. Trying to understand the economic forces that surround every society is what economists grapple with, forces so dynamic that they can lift an individual's standard of living to a higher plain or bring a person tumbling down to the lowest financial valley.

> Economic forces impact everything and everyone in a society.

The role of money in a society, government intervention in the business community, poverty and the distribution of income, profit maximization, the rapidly increasing movement toward economic survival based on international competition, productivity, labor-management relations, limitations of natural resources, inflation, recessions, government taxing and spending, interest rates, consumer spending, investment spending, and wealth creation represent some of the economic forces that exert a powerful influence upon a society. As these shifting economic forces pull societies in various directions an array of feelings is aroused within each member of a society. Feelings of intrigue, security, anxiety, doubt, and even despair can spring forth as a society is propelled toward a seemingly unpredictable and uncontrollable economic future.

The upward and downward movements of the economic forces that impact the economy are important because everyone is concerned with making a living and tapping into the goods and services that are produced. Individuals' economic successes and failures affect their self-image and their role in society. Economic prosperity and equality of opportunity are the seeds that bring forth a politically stable society where each individual has the opportunity to reach personal and professional goals through hard work.

Besides the impact upon our daily life, economic forces often intrigue us because of the seemingly mystical process by which the different economic variables come together in the marketplace and produce an economic environment in which no member of a society can escape. The economic environment, or economy, that engulfs a society can be described as a manmade entity that consists of all the income and production generated within a country.

In figure 4.1 the production of goods and services is represented by the upper portion of the diagram; income is represented by the lower portion. What the diagram illustrates is that within every economy the production of goods and services must equal the income generated from the production of those goods and services. Businesses produce the goods and services that are available within a society and households purchase those goods and services. Households provide businesses with the factors of production, and in return households eventually receive all the interest, wages, rent payments, and profits distributed. Therefore, production equals income, and it is the linkage between production and income that defines the structure (command versus market) and financial strength of an economy.

In today's world, the economy of each country impacts the economic performance of every other country. Thus, the world economy resembles

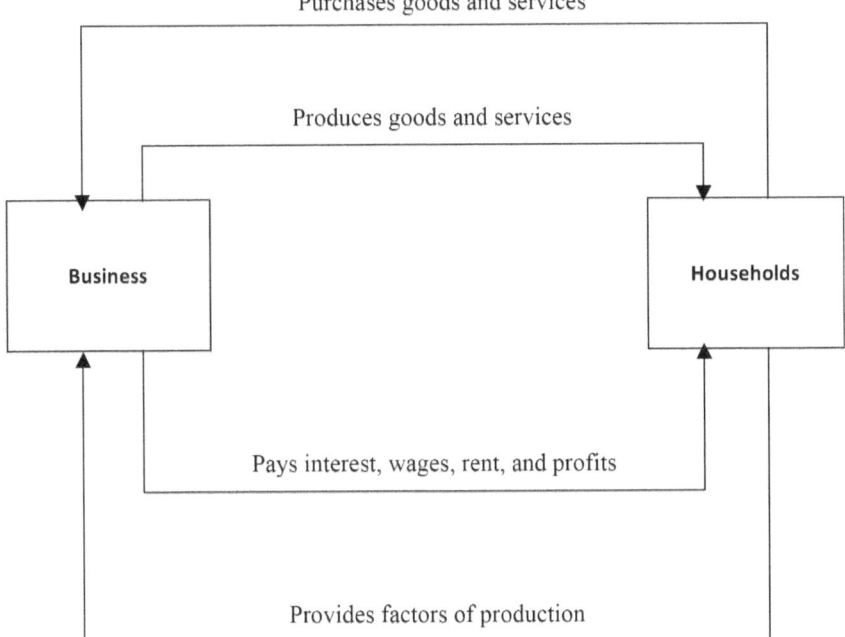

Figure 4.1. A Circular Flow Diagram of an Economy

a patchwork quilt, in which the economies of every country are woven together and form one giant economic community.

Because economic growth and production is so vital to a society, the health of the economy is constantly monitored for signs of strength and weakness. When the economy is strong, it serves as a life-line that keeps a society together. When the economy is weak, it can eventually act as a fuse that sets off an explosion of social unrest. Because of the connection between economic performance and social stability, economics and politics are bound together in a complex and often difficult relationship. The mixture of economics and politics is a courtship that will last forever as economists continue to search for answers regarding the inner workings of the economy, and politicians continue to use those answers in an attempt to gain some control over the economy and maintain authority over the society.

Economic forces within a society are capable of fostering an atmosphere of financial stability when the economy is growing, when wages are rising, when sales are expanding, when productivity is increasing, and when technology is advancing. These positive economic signals create a feeling that our lives, from an economic perspective, seem to be headed in the right direction. When a society feels secure about the economy, spending on goods and services tends to increase. A rise in spending results in an increase in production, which expands employment opportunities. When the economy is in an upward cycle, individuals feel confident about their economic situation and tend to have high expectations regarding the future.

On the flip side, economic forces create anxiety when the economy slows down and unemployment starts to rise, when inflation increases and consumer purchasing power is reduced, when sales and production begins to falter. Thus, a decline in economic performance reduces confidence in the economy. People start to worry about their jobs and wonder if their income will be enough to cover their expenses. Individuals cut back on spending, which reduces production and increases unemployment.

When the economy is in a downward cycle, the society looks toward the government and expects politicians to be able to bring an end to the downward motion of the economy. This is the time when political finger-pointing intensifies and social unrest starts to boil to the surface, threatening the structure of the society. If economic performance continues to deteriorate, the societal threads that hold a community together may come undone. Eventually, the society will collapse and fade into history.

The ups and downs of economic activity not only cause concern, but can easily create confusion over what is occurring within the economy. One of the main problems that economists face in forecasting economic conditions is the reality that the economy is in a constant state of flux and the data that is required to complete an analysis cannot be quickly collected. The lack of accurate and timely data makes the task of economic forecasting a risky business.

Another problem with economic forecasting is that economists cannot create a laboratory to examine cause-and-effect relationships among the various economic variables. Thus, the inability of economists to place an entire economy under a microscope causes a research void that hinders the ability of economists to accurately and consistently predict economic events.

How can we obtain permanent economic growth? How can we manage inflation? What is the key to increasing productivity in the manufacturing and service industries? How do individuals determine how much of their income to spend or save? What role should the government play in the economy? Gaining a complete answer to these economic questions is critical because the lifestyle people can achieve hinges upon the economic system that surrounds them, and how well that system is performing.

Since economic realities exert such a powerful influence upon every individual, a more in-depth understanding of economics can lead us toward a deeper understanding of ourselves, our society, and why the emphasis upon competition has become a philosophical movement in education.

ECONOMICS

The reality of our daily existence is that the relationship between economic phenomena and the lifestyle that an individual can achieve forms the centerpiece around which our lives are structured.

By gaining a better understanding of economics, we can also gain a better understanding of why the notion of competition among schools has gained a foothold in education.

Like a group of explorers seeking out the unknown, our quest to unmask the world of economics and its connection with education continues with the realization that the field of economics is a social science rather than a natural science. The natural sciences (also known as the physical sciences) investigate nature and the properties of material bodies and natural phenomena. The social sciences focus on investigating social phenomena, and in the final analysis, the social sciences are concerned with studying and analyzing human behavior.

Thus, the social sciences, for the most part, are not governed by any of the physical laws of nature. As a result, the social sciences have not been able to establish generalizations equivalent to the theories of the natural sciences in scope of explanatory power or in capacity to yield precise predictions.

Since economics is a social science, the economic phenomenon that is studied pertains to manmade forces that are not subject to the physical laws of nature. Does the inability to base economic theory upon physical or natural laws mean that economic research and theories are meaningless? Of course not, for it is only through research and the development of theories that a field of study can move forward toward the discovery of truth.

Research uncovers facts that lead to the discovery of additional facts. Through this discovery process, the building blocks of knowledge are compiled. As knowledge increases, humankind moves toward an understanding of the universal truths that shape our economic world. To uncover these truths, economic theories are developed on a macro and micro level.

Macroeconomics is concerned with the problems of economic growth, unemployment, and inflation. Each of these factors is an indicator of the overall state of the economy and how fully resources are utilized. By law, in the United States, the government has a macroeconomic responsibility for insuring that economic growth remains high and that unemployment and inflation remain low.

Through fiscal and monetary policies, the government of the United States seeks to ensure that these economic goals are attained. Monetary policy involves regulating the amount of money in circulation within an economy. The Federal Reserve is responsible for monetary policy. Fiscal policy relates to the taxing and spending policies of the government.

Microeconomics is concerned with individual products and decisions made by individual firms and consumers. Microeconomics digs beneath the macroeconomic picture to understand how economic activity occurs on an individual basis as opposed to a societal or aggregate analysis.

Both macroeconomic and microeconomic principles are rooted in a chain of reasoning that begins with the concept of scarcity. Recall from a previous chapter that scarcity refers to the premise that all resources are limited (scarce) while demands are unlimited. Because of scarcity, choices must be made, and tradeoffs exist. To produce more of one good or service requires lowering the production of another good or service. Economists use a production possibilities frontier to measure the amount of production that must be sacrificed of a good or service when the production of another good or service is increased.

Scarcity and production choices are best illustrated by the fundamental economic concepts of demand and supply. In a free-market society, economic decisions are determined by individual preferences in the marketplace; in other words, demand and supply govern economic outcomes. If there is a strong demand for a particular good or service, then that particular good or service will be produced or supplied. The higher demand for a particular good or service will lead to an increase in the quantity supplied of that good or service as the short run price increases. The purchase price establishes the monetary value associated with a particular good or service.

Money can be thought of as a commodity that plays several critical roles in an economy; for our purposes, we will focus on its role as a medium of exchange, meaning money can be traded directly for other commodities. Sellers are willing to take money in exchange for their product with the knowledge that as buyers, they can freely exchange the money for other commodities.

Money is the economic lubricant that keeps the financial engine of an economy running, and most of our daily routines are devoted toward earning the money that is necessary to purchase the goods and services we desire. The more value (or importance) a society associates with a particular occupation, the more money (income) an individual can receive.

The more income, the more goods and services an individual can afford. The more goods and services that are produced, the higher the production level for a society. Thus, the demand for, and supply of, goods and services drives production within a free-market society. Production then generates employment which provides the income to individuals so they can afford to purchase the goods and services that are produced.

Through demand and supply an equilibrium price will eventually be established in the marketplace, meaning that the price an individual wants to pay for a particular good or service will be the exact price that a producer wants to receive for manufacturing the product, or a retailer wants for selling the product, or a provider of a service wants for offering the service.

Price of a good

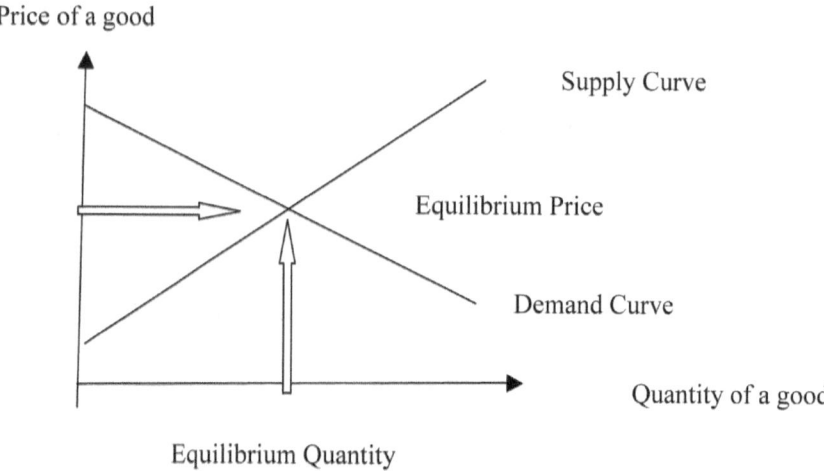

Figure 4.2. The Equilibrium Price Auction Model

Thus, the price and quantity demanded and supplied of a particular good or service are said to be in an equilibrium state. The equilibrium price auction model is utilized to illustrate an equilibrium state.

A supply curve is a graph of a supply schedule. It shows how the quantity supplied will change as the price changes, holding all other determinants of supply constant during a specific period of time. A demand curve is a graph of a demand schedule. It illustrates how the quantity demanded will change as the price changes, holding all other determinants of demand constant during a specific period of time. The equilibrium price represents the price at which the quantity demanded by consumers equals the quantity supplied by suppliers.

The most effective way to achieve equilibrium price and quantity is through the free market where competition among producers leads to an equilibrium state. Competition forces producers to provide products at the price, and the level of quality, demanded by the consumer.

It is the notion of how competition drives optimal outcomes in the equilibrium price auction model that creates a desire for charter schools and other educational alternatives to the traditional school system. Although the equilibrium price model is the best model for understanding the economic activity of a society, it's not the proper paradigm for understanding the educational process. The clarity that the equilibrium price auction model brings to the world of economics is lost in the educational arena. In the educational environment, reality is not about competition.

> ## NOT THE RIGHT FRAMEWORK
>
> The equilibrium price auction model and competition are the wrong paradigms for education.

So if it's not competition, what drives educational reality? The truth is educational performance rests upon cooperation and a focus on equal funding for all students, no matter where they attend school.

The key to a long-term school improvement strategy is to increase the internal capacity of each school, meaning developing highly interactive, collaborative, formal and informal systems in which teachers and administrators hold each other accountable for their actions vis-à-vis students (Elmore cited by Fullan, 2006, p. 27). Educational researcher Michael Fullan writes, "If we do not do something to increase the internal capacity of schools, we will spend the rest of our days mired in the awful-to-adequate stew of failed reform" (Fullan, 2006, p. 27).

Fullan further suggests that internal capacity building is framed upon three principles: (1) accountability, (2) collaboration, and (3) initiative. Accountability means sharing of information and obtaining accurate, timely feedback regarding student achievement. High levels of communication and respect between teachers and administration must be fostered, and the focus of the school must be upon high levels of student achievement. Collaboration means that everyone works together. People are willing to help each other and a sense of belonging is developed within the school. Initiative means that everyone in the school feels that their actions are meaningful and make a difference. Individuals taking initiative will result in improvements and innovations.

In his book, *Leadership and Sustainability*, Michael Fullan (2005) proposed the eight elements of sustainability as an overall framework for improving school performance and student learning. The eight elements are (1) public service with a moral purpose; (2) commitment to changing context at all levels; (3) lateral capacity; (4) intelligent accountability and vertical relationships; (5) deep learning; (6) dual commitment to short-term and long-term results; (7) cyclical energizing; and (8) the long lever of leadership.

Deeply embedded in the eight elements of sustainability are three notions. The first is capacity building which "involves developing the collective ability—dispositions, skills, knowledge, motivation, and resources—to act together to bring about positive change" (Fullan, 2005, p. 4). The second notion is context, which refers to the structure and cultures within which one works. According to Fullan changing a system "means changing the entire context within which people work" (Fullan, 2005, p. 16). The third notion is that systems thinking is required in today's interconnected global environment, for it provides an analytical approach that allows us to fully examine and appreciate the interdependency that an action has on an entire system, not just the immediate and local impact of an action (Richmond, 1991).

More specifically, public service with a moral purpose consists of three parts: (1) raising the bar and reducing the gap in student learning; (2) treating others with respect; and (3) changing the social environment for the better. In sum, we should act with a moral purpose.

Commitment to changing context at all levels refers to the structure and culture in which an individual works. The structure and culture must be aimed at increasing collaboration and focusing on student achievement. It should be clearly understood by all stakeholders that the main function of the school is to increase student achievement and any activity or function should support that main goal. The bottom line is to improve student performance.

Lateral capacity building through networks focuses on principals and teachers working with their peers from other schools and districts to improve individual school and district performance. Lateral capacity building is all about collaboration, not competition among schools

Intelligent accountability refers to the notion that at all levels the educational system should be infused with excellent data and ensure that school and district staff have the capacity to use the data so that everyone knows what effect the staff's actions are having on student learning and make adjustments when necessary.

Vertical relationships mean that everyone within the academic pipeline from the federal government level to the local school district should be communicating and working together to bring about continuous and sustainable student achievement.

Deep learning involves (1) reducing the fear of trying new ideas, concepts, and techniques that could have the potential for improving student achievement. "Governments must give active permission to schools to innovate and provide a climate in which failure can be given a different meaning. . . . Mistakes can be accepted or even encouraged, provided that they are a means of improvement"; (2) developing a learning community and organization; (3) promoting a love for learning on the part of all stakeholders.

Dual commitment to short-term and long-term results suggests that educational leaders need to demonstrate short-term and long-term successes in student achievement in order to build trust with their stakeholders. Once trust has been established, the stage is set for the development of a system-wide financial commitment to education.

Districts need to take two steps to increase financial investment. The first step is that they need to redeploy existing resources in the service of capacity building, focusing on teaching and learning; and secondly, districts need to figure out how to give responsive local and central governing bodies the confidence to risk investing additional money. Governments and schools must set challenging targets, take action to obtain early results, and intervene in situations of terrible performance all the while investing in the eight elements of sustainability. In sum, if we create a cycle where public education delivers results, the public gains confidence and is therefore willing to invest through taxation, and as a consequence the system is able to improve further.

Cyclical energizing refers to the fact that the eight elements of sustainability will require changes and challenges that can easily burn out an individual trying to bring about educational reforms. Burnout, turnover, and eroding morale are serious threats to achieving sustainability and the development of school cultures that enhance teacher and student performance. Leaders need to seek and harness four sources of energy: physical, emotional, mental, and spiritual. But instead of continually trying to maximize energy, cycles of high performance followed by recovery are required. Sustainability is cyclical, not linear. Periods where leaders push for greater accomplishments should be followed by a period of replenishment to avoid burnout.

The long lever of leadership focuses upon developing a group of leaders who become system thinkers and who work to implement all principles of sustainability and develop other leaders. Educational leaders must develop a pool of new leaders devoted to implementing the eight elements of sustainability and provide opportunities for personal growth and job challenges. The long lever of leadership is a continuous type of concept ranging from a conceptual aspect to a technical component. The conceptual aspect deals with "seeing the picture" of what is occurring that impacts the system, and the technical component focuses upon developing tools that capture the behavior being exhibited by the system in order to measure the output that is being produced by the system.

The bottom line regarding the eight elements of sustainability is that each principle is built upon the educational reality of cooperation. Cooperation within and among schools, and between school districts, fosters educational improvement.

Naturally flowing from an emphasis upon cooperation and the creation of a collaborative educational system is the educational reality of equal funding for all students. Although public schools can and will differ in many ways, one of the most important variables is per-pupil expenditure—the amount of money spent per student. Think of per-pupil expenditure as a financial package put together by local school boards with money received from the local, state, and federal governments (Alexander and Salmon cited by Newman, 2002, p. 347). The educational reality is that the quality of an educational experience depends upon the financial package put together.

Let's be clear, the educational reality is not about throwing more money toward education, but instead the reality is that per-pupil expenditure must be the same no matter where a student lives to ensure that each student has equal opportunities to learn. In sum, equal learning opportunities for each student are dependent upon equal funding per student.

THE CORRECT EDUCATIONAL PARADIGM

Cooperation, not competition, and equal funding per student

CRITICAL POINTS TO REMEMBER

- The reality of our daily existence is that the relationship between economic phenomena and the lifestyle that an individual can achieve forms the centerpiece around which our lives are structured.
- By gaining a better understanding of economics, we also gain a better understanding of why the notion of competition among schools has gained a foothold in education.
- Being able to handle the truth regarding education involves grasping the reality reflected in the following statements:
  - The clarity that the equilibrium price auction model brings to the world of economics and the importance of competition are lost in the educational arena. Therefore, the equilibrium price auction model and the emphasis upon competition are the wrong paradigms for education.
  - Educational reality is about cooperation and equal funding.
  - Cooperation within and among schools, and between school districts, leads to high educational outcomes.
  - When equal funding exists, it does not matter what type of school a student attends (traditional, charter, independent, and so forth) nor the location of the school because each student receives equal funding, and equal opportunities to learn. Equal funding levels the playing field across the board. Wealthier neighborhoods no longer have an advantage. The reality is that equal learning opportunities for each student depends upon equal funding per student.

REFERENCES

Alexander, K., and Salmon, R. (1995). *Public school finance in the United States.* Needham: MA: Allyn & Bacon.

Elmore, R. (2004). *School reform from the inside out: Policy, practice, and performance.* Cambridge, MA: Harvard University Press.

Fullan, M. (2005). *Leadership and sustainability: System thinkers in action.* Thousand Oaks, CA: Corwin Press/Sage Publications Company.

Fullan, M. (2006). *Turnaround leadership.* San Francisco: Jossey-Bass.

Newman, J. (2002). *America's teachers: An introduction to education.* Boston: Allyn & Bacon/Pearson Education Co.

Richmond, B. (1991). *Systems thinking: Four key questions.* Hanover, NH: High Performance Systems, Inc.

5

Lacking a Love for Learning

Learning is increasing one's knowledge, skills, and/or abilities, and putting it simply, if one does not have the desire to learn, learning will not be maximized. At the classroom level there are two primary actors: the teacher and the student. If either lacks the fire to continually engage in the learning process then it's quite clear what the outcome will be.

> **TEACHERS AND STUDENTS**
>
> Being able to handle the truth regarding education means being able to accept the fact that teachers and students need to love to learn to maximize the learning process.

In management literature, there is a theory that proposes that each employee is either an "X" or "Y" employee. An "X" employee is generally characterized as being lazy, and management must always prod that individual along or nothing will get accomplished. In other words, that employee is basically there to collect a paycheck and only does the minimum amount of work, if that. A theory "Y" employee is the opposite of a theory "X" employee. Theory "X" and "Y" employees are like matter and antimatter, one is the reverse of the other.

Let's expand the theory "X" and "Y" model to the classroom by assuming there are theory "X" and theory "Y" students and teachers. A theory "X" student doesn't want anything to do with school or learning. Basically the same thing can be said about a theory "X" teacher. This type of teacher never voluntarily engages in professional development activities and will only learn something new when forced to do so.

Theory "Y" students and teachers are the opposite of theory "X" students and teachers. Theory "Y" students and teachers love learning and are highly engaged in the learning process. Given theory "X" and "Y" students and teachers, the level of learning that will occur within the classroom can be illustrated by the matrix in figure 5.1.

When a classroom consists of a theory "X" student and teacher, the learning outcome will be "XX" or minimum at best. On the opposite side of the coin, if the classroom consists of both a theory "Y" teacher and student then the learning outcome will be maximized. If the classroom consists of a theory "X" teacher and a theory "Y" student, the learning outcome will be better than minimum, but less than optimal; however, an optimal learning outcome is still possible. Finally, if the teacher is a theory "Y" teacher and the student is a theory "X" student, the learning outcome will most likely be minimized, unless the teacher can transform the student into a theory "Y" student.

The most important aspect of the matrix is the focus upon reality. A great teacher cannot get optimal outcomes from theory "X" students. A theory "Y" student will have to work very hard, mostly on his or her own, to get a better than minimum learning outcome if that student has to contend with a theory "X" teacher. To understand why this is true, one needs to recognize the fact that the responsibility for learning is the student's. That's why a theory "Y" student can overcome a theory "X" teacher, and a theory "Y" teacher might be able to create an optimal learning out-

		Teacher	
		X	Y
Student	X	XX	XY (YY- possible)
	Y	XY (YY- possible)	YY

Figure 5.1.

come, but that will only be possible if the theory "X" student becomes a theory "Y" student. Theory "X" students will always minimize learning outcomes.

To summarize, when considering only the teacher and the student, the learning that takes place in a classroom will always be optimal when a theory "Y" teacher and a theory "Y" student are in the classroom. Learning will always be minimized when a classroom consists of both a theory "X" teacher and student. Between these two extremes, the quality of the learning experience will probably be less than optimal.

Beneath the "visible" learning outcomes that take place within a classroom are the theories upon which the process of learning occurs:

- *Reinforcement theory* emphasizes that people are motivated to perform or avoid certain behaviors because of past outcomes that have resulted from those behaviors. From an educational perspective, reinforcement theory suggests that for learners to acquire knowledge, change their behavior, or modify skills, the teacher needs to identify what outcomes the learner perceives as being positive (or negative). Teachers then need to link these outcomes to learners who need or want to acquire knowledge or skills or improved abilities.
- *Social learning theory* suggests that learners first watch others who act as models. In an educational scenario, a group of students can be presented with models of effective behaviors (e.g., performing proper social behavior) and told about the relationship between these desirable behaviors and their various consequences (such as praise, or improving social relationships). Students then rehearse the behaviors and experience the consequences, building cognitive maps that intensify the links and set the stage for future behaviors. The learning impact occurs when the subject tries the behavior and experiences a positive result.
- *Goal-setting theory* implies that establishing and committing to specific and challenging goals can influence an individual's behavior. From an educational perspective, setting goals can help a student identify the specific outcomes that should be achieved from the learning situation.
- *Need theories* (Maslow's hierarchy of needs, Alderfer's ERG theory, Herzberg's dual-structure theory, and David McClelland's need

theory) assume that need deficiencies cause behavior. Need theories suggest that to motivate learners, teachers should identify student needs and communicate how the academic program content relates to fulfilling those needs.
- *Expectancy theory* implies that an individual's behavior is a function of three factors (expectancy, instrumentality, and valence). The *expectancy* factor refers to an individual's belief that the effort will lead to a particular performance level; that the performance level is associated with a particular outcome (instrumentality factor); and that the outcome is valued by the individual (valence factor). From an educational perspective, expectancy theory suggests that learning is most likely to occur when students believe they can learn the content of the program (expectancy); when learning is linked to an outcome, such as better grade (instrumentality); and when students value the outcomes.

With an understanding of the various learning theories and using them as a guide for improving the educational environment, theory "Y" teachers can set the stage for optimal learning. As for theory "X" teachers and students, as with anything else associated with learning, they have no interest in improving their knowledge, skills, and (or) abilities.

CRITICAL POINTS TO REMEMBER

- Learning is increasing one's knowledge, skills, and/or abilities—period.
- Theory "Y" teachers and students love to learn.
- Theory "Y" teachers will utilize learning theories to help improve the learning environment.
- Theory "X" teachers and students minimize learning outcomes.
- Being able to handle the truth regarding education means being able to accept the fact that teachers and students need to love to learn to maximize the learning process.

6

Students Are Part of the Problem

U.S. students get the top score for sleepiness in the classroom. Teachers report that student sleepiness limits instructional time in the classroom (Yettick, 2014). Yeah, our students are at the top of the list; let's give everyone a gold star.

> Being able to handle the truth regarding education means acknowledging the reality that only those students willing to put forth the time and effort that is required to learn will maximize their learning.

Whether it's sleepiness or just plain lack of effort and motivation, the student is a major problem in the learning process. The attitudes and behavior of many students directly lead to their underachievement, or in a worst-case scenario, their own failure. That's the truth, hard as it is to accept. Those not willing to face this reality will continue down the path of proposing the latest silver bullet solution and blaming everything other than the student. Let's be clear, the kind of student that is a major hindrance to educational progress is the theory "X" student, the individual who is lazy, unmotivated, and uninterested in school and learning.

What sense would it make for a doctor who has a patient with cancer to blame the diagnostic equipment for the situation? It's the cancer that's killing the patient. So why blame the teacher and the educational process for a student who does not want to be any part of the educational system? Individuals must be held accountable for the decisions they make in life. If someone does not want to learn, he or she is not going to learn. Learning takes time and enormous effort. For those who choose not to put forth the time and effort, what level of learning can occur?

The fact of the matter is, students can be divided along two extremes: those who have made the decision to be highly engaged in the learning process and those who haven't; actual learning outcomes will occur somewhere between those two extremes. Students who put forth the effort increase the probability of higher achievement; those who don't will achieve less. It's that simple.

The reality of the learning process is that the student holds the key to the level of success or failure that will result. Those who want to succeed will do whatever it takes and overcome any obstacles because they have the passion to improve themselves. Ultimately, learning is about improving yourself whether it's your knowledge, skills, or abilities. Only those individuals who want to improve themselves are willing to put forth the effort.

How ironic it is that the student, who can be such a major problem for the learning process, is in the end a critical part of the solution. In a strange way, it's comforting to understand the power that a student has in his or her learning. Yes, there are failing educational systems and other societal issues, but the person who is truly seeking self-improvement still holds the key to his or her self-discovery. Every day, rags-to-riches stories unfold. That's the beauty of living in a society where a person, no matter what his or her educational background, can still overcome many disadvantages.

The role of the educational system is to reduce obstacles and inspire a love for learning. However, the key to educational success ultimately lies with the student, for each one must make the decision to want to learn, no matter what he or she faces. Quite simply, the learning process depends upon a commitment to learning.

Certainly coming from a wealthier school district increases the probability of a better outcome, but many students who have the best of everything settle for mediocre outcomes because they don't have the fire inside of them to want to learn. That hunger for learning is replaced by other priorities. Learning requires that an individual prioritize learning first, and everything else second.

Sorry, but reality is often difficult to accept.

CRITICAL POINTS TO REMEMBER

- The student is a major problem and a major portion of the solution, in terms of what will be learned in the classroom.
- Only those students willing to put forth the time and effort that is required to learn will maximize their learning.

REFERENCES

Yettick, H. (2014, June 11). U.S. students get top scores for sleepiness. *Education Week,* pp. 1, 20.

7

Bad Teachers

In big-city school districts, 16 percent of teachers are chronically absent from the classroom, with a range of 40 percent in Buffalo, New York, to 5 percent in Indianapolis (National Council on Teacher Education, 2014). These teachers give great teachers a bad rap.

Not only can an individual teacher be a bad teacher, the environment (or organizational culture) that surrounds the teacher has an impact on the effectiveness of the teaching situation, just as ocean currents influence the movement of a ship. Sometimes the current is flowing in the same direction as the ship; other times, the current pounds the ship, making the journey a more difficult one.

Ultimately, it is the vastness of the ocean that defines how a day's sail is going to turn out, and the same can be said about an organization's culture, because the culture of an organization sets the parameters by which things get done (Deal and Kennedy, 1982). The culture of an organization consumes everything within the organization; all organizational tasks are accomplished within the boundaries set by the culture. Like a lonely ship on the ocean, an individual within an organization can only accomplish so much given the constraints imposed upon the individual by the culture that dominates the organization.

TEACHING

Handling the truth regarding education requires an examination of the environment in which a teacher operates.

School culture has been defined as shared norms, values, beliefs, and attitudes that promote mutual caring and trust among all members (Leithwood and Riehl, 2003). In other words, school culture is the collective work patterns of a system (or school) as perceived by the staff members (Johnson and Snyder, 1996). Notice that Johnson and Snyder do not assume that the culture of a school naturally leads to an atmosphere of trust among the members of the school. Only school cultures that build trust among administrators, staff, and faculty increase the probability of establishing an effective student learning environment.

Besides building an atmosphere of trust, another aspect of an effective student learning culture includes actively engaging parents and students in the learning process (Taylor and Pearson, 1999). Thompson (2004) advocates that an effective school is a learning organization that continually adapts to a changing environment and is never satisfied with the status quo. As stated by Senge (1990), organizations that discover how to tap people's commitment and ability to learn will be the organizations that thrive in the future.

A more complete characterization of an effective learning environment is the school-based management approach (SBM). The SBM model suggests that an effective school environment consists of eight elements: (a) a vision focused on teaching and learning that is coordinated with student learning standards, (b) site-based decision-making authority to create meaningful change in teaching and learning, (c) broadly dispersed power authority, (d) a professional learning community, (e) an established network for communicating information to all stakeholders, (f) monetary and nonmonetary rewards to individuals and groups that achieve school goals, (g) school leadership shared among administration and teachers, and (h) cultivated resources (Briggs and Wohlstetter, 2003).

If we sweep aside the various descriptions of what constitutes an effective school culture, like shoveling the snow off of a driveway so that a clear path to the street can be laid out, what binds school culture and teaching effectiveness together is the notion of teacher isolation versus collegiality.

Collegiality among teachers pertains to the frequency of communication and mutual support that teachers receive from each other (and the administration) in terms of improving pedagogy and student achievement. Collegiality is embedded in the concept of professional learning communities (PLCs), collaborative work cultures, or learning-enriched schools.

> Collegiality is the key to a school culture focused upon teacher effectiveness and a professional learning community.

In a PLC, the assumption is that improvements in teaching are a collective activity rather than an individual enterprise. Teachers working with other teachers in terms of analyzing, evaluating, and experimenting set the conditions under which teachers improve (Rosenholtz cited by Fullan, 2007). The elements of PLCs are (1) a focus on learning, (2) a collaborative learning environment (culture) for all, (3) a collective pursuit of best practices as well as a commitment to continuous improvement, and (4) a focus on results (Dufour et al. cited by Fullan, 2007). The main roadblocks to establishing PLCs include (1) policy makers, administrators, and school cultures that inhibit collaboration, as well as (2) teachers that resist opening up their classroom to colleagues (Fullan, 2007).

When moving from the culture of a school to the classroom, the focus shifts to the teacher. With the spotlight solely upon the teacher and the classroom, a critical attribute of a great teacher is the ability to be an effective communicator. A teacher's ability to effectively communicate information to students is becoming more critical every day as demographic conditions continue to dramatically shift in the United States.

Given a rapidly changing demographic environment, "Cultural values and beliefs are at the center of students' responses to teachers' strategies and of students' own attempts to engage in and influence interactions in the classroom" (Rothstein-Fisch and Trumbull, 2008, p. xiii). Although many teachers recognize differences in student learning styles, many do not know how to apply this knowledge to change the atmosphere of their classrooms (Sullivan and Buttner cited by Kaenzig, Hyatt, and Anderson, 2007).

To put it simply, presenting information in order to maximize the learning process starts with a desire on the part of a teacher to want to be in the classroom and actively engaged with the students. Excellent teachers examine the learning goals that a student chooses since that selection process is influenced by the cultural background and life experiences of the student, especially the students' perceptions of their capability to handle a particular learning task.

A student's self-efficacy affects her motivation, choice of goals, expectations of success, and attributions for success or failure. A student with high levels of self-efficacy tends to select task mastery goals or do what is necessary to learn the information and skills required to accomplish the learning task. Performance-approach goals tend to also be selected by students with high levels of self-efficacy since these students are interested in demonstrating to their teachers and peers their intellectual capability to outperform most other students.

On the other hand, students with low levels of self-efficacy tend to select performance-avoidance goals, which involve reducing the possibility of failure by avoiding novel and challenging tasks or cheating. In addition, students with low levels of self-efficacy may engage in self-handicapping behaviors in order to blame performance outcomes on the circumstances rather than on their ability. What can be summarized regarding self-efficacy is that students with high levels of self-efficacy expect positive educational outcomes and attribute the outcome to their own ability and effort; the opposite is true for students with low levels of self-efficacy.

Gaining an understanding of a student's level of self-efficacy and how a student's culture and life experiences influence his expectations of academic success or failure leads to the realization that quality teaching is twofold: subject-matter expertise and pedagogy—the art of presenting subject matter content. Too often teachers get so wrapped up in presenting the body of knowledge, pedagogy is a minor consideration. Teachers simply toss information to the students and basically leave it to them to sort through the complexity and try to make sense of the material. Students with a low level of self-efficacy are lost in the process, left behind, and ultimately forgotten.

Great teachers (Theory "Y") are student centered, meaning that pedagogy is as important as subject matter expertise. Students have different learning styles or preferences for dealing with intellectual tasks as well as different practical, creative, and analytical abilities. To make sure that students from all social-class, gender, racial, language, and cultural groups have an equal opportunity to learn in the classroom, teachers need to understand that a variety of teaching methodologies must be utilized. Various teaching methodologies include:

- The collaborative problem-solving approach (CPS). The CPS approach has two components: problem-based learning and collaborative learning. Problem-based learning involves presenting students with a problem scenario. The students then work together in a collaborative effort to solve the problem.
- Service learning links academic course work with community service projects with the objective of improving each student's self-perception as well as fostering an appreciation of teamwork. As part of the service-learning project students are expected to identify issues, explore theories, and provide evidence relating their experiences to various theories.
- Lecturing has its place in a teacher's repertoire; however, to maximize student learning, the lecture method must not be exclusively utilized.
- Good lecturing in combination with student-centered learning activities or active student participation offers a positive learning alternative to the straightforward lecture method.
- Role-play simulations challenge students to process information efficiently, to apply analytical techniques, to sharpen decision-making skills, and to improve their negotiation skills.
- The inverted classroom approach means that activities that have traditionally occurred inside the classroom can now take place outside the classroom and vice versa. For example, lectures can be viewed outside of the classroom on a DVD while end-of-chapter questions usually assigned as homework can become the focal point within the classroom.
- Case studies examining a variety of situations can be utilized in the classroom to develop analytical and reasoning skills.

- Technology-based teaching methodologies such as DVDs, CDs, various computer technologies, and the Internet can be utilized to promote student academic success and understanding of the subject matter being explored.

Incorporating effective teaching methodologies in the classroom is a vital component of the learning process and in most cases, acknowledging this truism is what separates the excellent teachers (Theory "Y") from the bad ones (Theory "X").

In the final analysis, there is no room for bad teachers in the educational system. The role of the teacher is to ensure that the subject matter being taught is communicated in an effective manner. This involves utilizing a variety of teaching methodologies and equipment in an attempt to create an atmosphere that promotes learning. Quality teaching encourages students to develop a lifelong passion for learning and to never blindly follow an ideology. Learning should be about uncovering facts that relate to complex issues.

Great teachers establish a positive classroom environment in which everyone is respected and encouraged to pursue excellence.

CRITICAL POINTS TO REMEMBER

- Given that the implicit goal of a school is to provide a quality learning experience and that teacher performance is a primary factor that impacts the learning environment, it's critical to examine the impact of school culture upon teacher performance.
- Effective school cultures are focused upon collegiality, not teacher isolation.
- Teachers must recognize that their primary goal is to establish a learning environment in which the body of knowledge is presented in an effective manner that includes utilizing a variety of teaching methodologies.
- Education is about expanding knowledge and improving student learning, period. Understanding the cultural and life experiences of students and focusing upon the individual learning characteristics of students cause teachers to consider the pedagogies they utilize in the classroom. Teachers who adjust their teaching styles to the needs of

the students have begun the process of enhancing the learning environment. An effective learning environment should be the ultimate goal for all teachers.

REFERENCES

Briggs, K., and Wohlstetter, P. (2003). Key elements of a successful school-based management strategy. *School Effectiveness and School Improvement* 14, 351–72.

Deal, T., and Kennedy, A., (1982). *Corporate cultures: The rites and rituals of corporate life.* Reading, MA: Addison-Wesley.

Dufour, R., Dufour, R., Eaker, R., and Many, T. (2006). *Learning by doing: A handbook for professional learning communities at work.* Bloomington, IN: Solution Tree

Fullan, M. (2007). *The new meaning of educational change* (4th ed.). New York: Teachers College Press.

Johnson W., and Snyder, K. (1996). School work culture and productivity. *Journal of Experimental Education* 64, 139–57.

Kaenzig, R., Hyatt, E., and Anderson, S. (2007). Gender differences in college of business educational experiences. *Journal of Education for Business* 83(2), 95–100.

Leithwood, K., and Riehl, C. (2003, January). What we know about successful school leadership. Accessed August, 21, 2005. www.cepa.gse.rutgers.edu/whatweknow.pdf.

National Council on Teacher Quality. (2014, June 11). Teacher-absence rates found to vary across big-city school districts. *Education Week*, p. 5.

Rothstein-Fisch, C., and Trumbull, E. (2008). *Managing diverse classrooms: How to build on students' cultural strengths.* Alexandria, VA: Association for Supervision and Curriculum Development (ASCD).

Senge, P. (1990). *The fifth discipline: The art and practice of the learning organization.* New York: Doubleday/Currency.

Sullivan, S., and Buttner, E. (1992). Changing more than the plumbing: Integrating women and gender differences into management and organizational behavior courses. *Journal of Management Education* 16, 76–89.

Taylor, B., and Pearson, D. (1999). Effective schools/accomplished teachers. *Reading Teacher* 53, 156–60.

Thompson, D. (2004). Organizational learning in action: Becoming an inviting school. *Journal of Invitational Theory and Practice* 10, 52–72.

8

The Myth about Maximizing Student Learning

> Realizing that education is a unique product is a step forward in terms of handling the truth regarding education.

From a microeconomic perspective, education is an unusual product, for it does not fit into any of the standard product markets: (1) a perfectly competitive market, (2) a monopoly, (3) a monopolistic competitive environment, or (4) an oligopoly. Given this situation, there is no microeconomic framework that applies to education. The fact that revenue is derived from the public through government taxing and spending as well as market sources (tuition and private contributions) leads to a unique set of economic and managerial challenges involving pricing and output decisions, as well as strategic planning objectives.

In addition, education does not fit into the traditional business input-output model. Nor do students fit the classic customer role. The lack of a functioning microeconomic model tends to explain why educators run from one fad to the next, wasting scarce financial and human resources. In the end, it is the students who suffer, and society is forced to pick up the tab for lost opportunities. Given the lack of a formal microeconomic model for education, many suggestions are routinely offered that provide piecemeal analysis and ideological interpretations regarding the structure of education and the learning process.

As noted by Back and Monroe (1985) and Jensen (1995) the conclusion by Coleman et al. (1966) that the socioeconomic factors of a student have more impact upon student performance than any other factor prompted an explosion of research aimed at identifying an effective school. The search to improve student performance intensified again in the early 1980s after the National Commission on Excellence in Education (1983) warned "that poor-quality schools were a threat to the nation's security" (Seyfarth, 2005, p. 3). The warning prompted the federal and state governments to actively examine and institute methodologies, practices, and policies to improve the quality of instruction throughout the P–12 educational pipeline.

Unfortunately, despite all the attempts to improve student achievement, it appears that student achievement continues to decline. Thomas Sowell (1993) stated that like many other people, he has long been appalled by the low quality and continuing deterioration of American education and that, given the counterproductive fads, fashions, and dogmas of American education, he was surprised that educational results are not even worse than they are.

The problems with public education and the associated financial and non-financial costs to society are reported daily in various publications. High school students haven't achieved any significant gains in reading or math for approximately four decades (Tomsho, 2009). A total of 41 percent of students entering community colleges and 29 percent of all entering college students are not prepared in at least one of the basic skills of reading, writing, and math (Byrd and MacDonald, 2005). As stated by Lagemann (2009), students are not being taught the basics well, nor are they being challenged intellectually because many schools are dreary places with too many youngsters dropping out.

In 1982, Brookover, Beamer, Efthim, Hathaway, Lezotte, Miller, Passalacqua, and Tornatzky wrote the book *Creating Effective Schools: An Inservice Program for Enhancing School Learning Climate and Achievement*. This groundbreaking work provided a framework for understanding what constitutes an effective school. The notion of an effective school is embedded in the concept of an effective school learning climate. A school learning climate is defined as "the norms, beliefs and attitudes reflected in institutional patterns and behavior practices that enhance or impede student learning" (Lezotte et al., 1980, p. 4).

EFFECTIVE SCHOOLS

Effective schools have an effective school learning climate.

According to Brookover et al. (1982), "an effective school learning climate refers to the particular characteristics and patterns of attitudes, beliefs, norms, role definitions, structure, and instructional behaviors which are associated with high achieving effective schools" (p. 25). Schools with effective learning climates may be classified under three headings: the ideology of the school, the organization of the school, and the instructional practices of the school. School ideology "refers to the general beliefs, norms, expectations, and feelings that characterize the school social system.

The belief that students can learn and that teachers can teach is an important characteristic of an effective school learning environment. This belief must also be associated with the staff's expectation that students can and will achieve at high levels. The expectations for students become generalized into norms, or standards of achievement" (Brookover et al., 1982, p. 3).

The organization of the school refers to the fact that many schools separate students into different tracks, different sections, or different groups in which a substantial proportion of students are classified as unable to learn as much as other students. A school in which a large proportion of the students do not achieve at very high levels is not an effective school (Brookover et al., 1982).

Instructional practices of an effective school are "characterized by clearly recognized and accepted objectives which are common for all students, plus a directed instructional program that is designed for all students to master those objectives" (Brookover et al., 1982, p. 5). Schools with an effective school learning culture are effective schools. An effective school "produces a high level of achievement for all students, regardless of family background" (Brookover et al., 1982, pp. 24–25).

In sum, according to Brookover et al. (1982), the following points capture the essence of the concept of a school learning climate. First, "a school learning climate relates to student achievement and those factors within a school that affect achievement" (Brookover et al., 1982, p. 25). Second, a school learning climate is the set of attitudes, beliefs, and behaviors within a building that collectively form the group norms of a school. Group norms tend to be maintained over time with new members being socialized into the prevailing sets of behaviors (Brookover et al., 1982). Third, schools are social systems and as such share some commonalities in learning climates.

However, schools also have different philosophies, instructional practices, beliefs, and expectations regarding student learning outcomes. Consequently, the variances in school learning climate produce different levels of student achievement. Finally, a school learning climate can change, and it's the members of the school social group who are the change agents. "Outsiders are unlikely to have much impact on the social group unless that group desires or is willing to change" (Brookover et al., 1982, p. 26).

Another approach to creating a positive school environment was proposed by the Association for Effective Schools (1996) in a document that summarized the school variables that have a high correlation with student performance. The variables are:

- "A clearly articulated mission statement through which staff and faculty share a common understanding of instructional goals, priorities, assessment measures, and a commitment to accepting responsibility for students' learning of the school's essential curricular goals." (Association for Effective Schools, 1996, p. 1)
- High academic expectations. All students are expected to master the essential course content and skills and the staff also believes that they have the ability to assist student achievement.
- Principals acting as instructional leaders by applying the characteristics of instructional effectiveness in the management of the instructional program.
- Frequent monitoring of student progress by utilizing a variety of assessment procedures.
- Teachers allocating a significant amount of classroom time to learning essential content and skills; high time-on-task classroom environment.
- Orderly and safe school environment.

- School officials should actively communicate the mission of the school to the parents and provide them with an opportunity to help the school achieve its mission.

In 2003, Thompson "depicted what he called a high-performance school system with eight features that have been shown to contribute to increasing student achievement" (Seyfarth, 2005, p. 5). The features are:

- A standards-based approach in which challenging standards are developed that specify what students should know and be able to accomplish.
- Adoption of a mission statement that enables "all students to meet challenging standards and develops policies and procedures for managing budgets and human resources that contribute to that goal." (Seyfarth, 2005, p. 5)
- A school climate that promotes a nurturing, supportive, respectful relationships with all stakeholders.
- School assessment that can be utilized to provide prompt and targeted assistance to underperforming schools.
- Professional development that's ongoing and provides high-quality professional development opportunities for all employees.
- Resources, including personnel, time, materials, and funds, first and foremost allocated in such a way as to support instructional practices.
- Data collection techniques and systems developed for the purpose of improving instructional practices and outcomes.
- Communication to internal and external stakeholders occurring on a regular basis. The communication should keep all stakeholders abreast of the schools' performance and invite their participation in decisions impacting school programs, policies, and practices.

At the core of these approaches is that educational structure and performance should focus upon the word "engagement." All successful education must end up engaging the hearts and minds of students (Fullan, 2007). To better engage students, changing teaching in the classroom involves "assessment for learning," meaning engaging students by utilizing data on learning performance to alter learning keyed to the needs of the individual (Fullan, 2007). Changing the way students participate in shaping the culture of a school might begin by inviting students "to talk about what makes learning difficult for them, about what diminishes their motivation and engagement, and what makes some give up and others settle for a 'minimum risk, minimum effort' position—even though they know that doing well matters" (Rudduck et al., cited by Fullan, 2007, p. 183).

Closely connected with student engagement is parent involvement in the educational process. The bottom line regarding parent involvement is that teachers and administrators must constantly speak "about the impor-

Figure 8.1. The Educational and Learning Reality Cycle. (What the Educational System Can Actually Accomplish)

tance of respecting parents, regardless of their background or education achievement" (Bryk and Schneider cited by Fullan, 2007, p. 193). Parents must be viewed as part of the learning solution.

Given the research regarding effective schools, student engagement, and parent involvement, what's the reality regarding what the educational system can actually accomplish? The fact is that the educational system can never maximize student learning, the educational system can only maximize the learning environment. The educational system can only control the factors within its system; variables outside of the educational system, such as the willingness of a student to want to be engaged in the learning process and the financial and emotional support a student receives from his or her family, impact educational outcomes.

As the saying goes, "You can lead a horse to water, but you can't make it drink." Students (and families) who have little or no interest in the educational system will negatively influence educational performance. The educational slogan that all students will be high achievers is a myth, and the educational system should not be judged by a myth.

What I call the Educational and Learning Reality Cycle (Wentland, 2013) demonstrates that student learning will only be maximized if the student is willing to put forth the required time and effort. Secondary to the level of effort exerted by the student is the family and cultural support that surrounds the student. The educational system can only maximize the structural environment.

CRITICAL POINTS TO REMEMBER

- Education does not conform to any microeconomic product market or the traditional input/output of business and therefore creates unique analysis challenges.
- The educational system can only maximize the learning environment.
- Students (and families) who have little or no interest in the educational system will negatively influence educational performance.
- The educational slogan that all students will be high achievers is a myth, and the educational system should not be judged by a myth.

- Given reality, the Educational and Learning Reality Cycle illustrates what the educational system can actually accomplish. Can you handle this educational fact?

REFERENCES

Association for Effective Schools, Inc. (1996). Correlates of effective schools. Retrieved February 14, 2006, from EBSCOhost research database.

Back, J., and Monroe, E. (1985). The effective schools concept: An effective way to help schools make a difference? [Electronic version]. *Education* 105(3), 232–36.

Brookover, W., Beamer, L., Efthim, H., Hathaway, D., Lezotte, L., Miller, S., Passalacqua, J., and Tornatzky, L. (1982). *Creating effective schools: An inservice program for enhancing school learning climate and achievement.* Holmes Beach, FL: Learning Publications, Inc.

Bryk, A., and Schneider, B. (2002). *Trust in schools.* New York: Russell Sage.

Coleman, J., Campbell, E., Hobson, C., McPartland, J., Mood, A., Weinfeld, F., and York, R. (1966). *Equality of educational opportunity.* Washington, DC: U.S. Government Printing Office.

Fullan, M. (2007). *The new meaning of educational change* (4th ed.). New York: Teachers College Press.

Lagemann, E. C. (January 21, 2009). Toward a national consensus. *Education Week,* pp. 28, 44.

Lezotte, L., Hathaway, D., Miller, S., Passalacqua, J., and Brookover, W. (1980). *School learning climate and student achievement: A social systems approach to increased student learning.* Tallahassee, FL: National Teacher Corps, Florida State University Foundation.

National Commission on Excellence in Education. (1983). *A nation at risk: The imperative for educational reform.* Washington, DC: U.S. Government Printing Office.

Rudduck, J., Chaplain, R., and Wallace, G. (1996). *School improvement: What can pupils tell us?* London: David Fulton.

Seyfarth, J. (2005). *Human resources management for effective schools* (4th ed.). Boston: Allyn & Bacon/Pearson Education, Inc.

Sowell, T. (1993). *Inside American education: The decline, the deception, the dogmas.* New York: The Free Press.

Thompson, S. (2003). A high-performance school system. In F. M. Duffy, *Courage, passion, and vision* (pp. 101–12). Lanham, MD: Scarecrow Press.

Tomsho, R. (April 29, 2009). Few gains are seen in high school test. *Wall Street Journal*, p. A5.
Wentland, Daniel. (2013). *Reality and education: A new direction for educational policy*. Lanham, MD: Rowman & Littlefield.

9

A Disconnection in the Educational Pipeline

> **EDUCATIONAL PIPELINE (P–16)**
>
> P–16 refers to preschool through undergraduate level of education and there are serious disconnections throughout the educational pipeline. Given this disconnection, no one should be surprised that student performance is subpar. That's the truth regarding education, can you handle it?

The quality of education throughout the P–16 educational pipeline should be a vital concern not only for the students that are directly impacted, but for all members of society. Economists continually stress how productivity is a critical key to personal and societal well-being. Providing quality education is a fundamental factor that determines whether a society will be able to achieve a high level of productivity and thus enjoy the material benefits that result from advances in productivity. An increase in productivity equates to an increase in national income, which culminates in a higher gross domestic product (GDP) per capita or a real improvement in the standard of living obtained by the members of a society, ceteris paribus.

Naik (2006) reported that China's massive financial investment in education has been bearing fruit: "China is increasingly making its mark with scientific discoveries and patents held by scientists" (Naik, 2006, p. A2). Even though the United States remains an R&D powerhouse, financial and capital investments by other countries in education and R&D represent a constant challenge to its productivity rate and thus the standard of living currently enjoyed by U.S. citizens (Naik, 2006). In sum, those countries that are productive succeed in a capitalistic economic environment; those countries that are not productive will not achieve a high standard of living (Mankiw, 2007).

> Productivity is the key to a higher standard of living and education is a driver of productivity.

Given the connection between education and productivity, the role that educational leaders play throughout the educational pipeline should be of concern because the quality of leadership impacts educational outcomes. The managerial principles and daily practices of educational leaders form the framework upon which the educational system is governed. In the final analysis, educational leadership principles are a critical piece of the puzzle that connects what happens in elementary and secondary education with what is required in higher education.

Today, the managerial principles that guide most training programs in educational leadership are the Interstate School Leaders Licensure Consortium standards (ISLLC). The preparation of high school students for college should involve all six of the ISLLC standards. The first standard focuses upon developing an academic vision that is shared and supported by all local school stakeholders. The second standard stresses that school culture and instructional programs should be conducive to student achievement and professional development of the faculty and staff. Standard three revolves around developing a safe, efficient, and effective school environment. The fourth standard relates to building a collaborative relationship with local stakeholders. Standard five pertains to ethical conduct. The sixth standard requires an awareness of the larger cultural, legal, economic, political, and social forces that impact the educational process.

Given the impact of education on productivity and one's ability to achieve a better quality of life, how are high schools doing in terms of student readiness for college? The issues voiced by many college and university presidents and faculty members regarding the preparedness of high school students for higher education can be summarized utilizing the ISLLC standards.

In regard to the first ISLLC standard, today there is no consistent vision or complete commitment to harmonizing what high schools expect of their graduates with what universities expect of their freshmen (Finn, 2006). In many cases this lack of a coherent vision between secondary and higher education is a consequence of not having a single definition of what is meant by college readiness (Haycock, Reed, and Thornton, 2006).

In regard to the second ISLLC standard, high-performing schools focus upon improving instruction because of the direct link with student achievement (Keller, 2007). Keller further commented that "successful school systems set high learning standards for their schools and move in when they are not met" (p. 8). Finally, according to Keller, establishing a high-quality teaching situation for every child must be at the heart of school improvement. As for professional development, Hunefeld (2009) stated that "teachers don't improve by listening to someone tell them how to do something newer or better in their classrooms" (p. 24). Instead, Hunefeld suggests that the way teachers learn is "by working together to address problems they themselves identify in their classrooms" (p. 24). This type of professional development is called collaborative professional development (PD).

In regard to the third ISLLC standard, "State and federal policy makers should rethink student-aid programs to create incentives for young people to apply themselves in high school, not just go through the motions" (Finn, 2006, B42). Finn further proposed that state operating subsidies for higher education should only pay for college-level work, not remediation, and that the K–12 school systems should be billed by the colleges for any remediation costs. Thus remediation costs will ultimately be borne by local school districts and the taxpayers that fund those ineffective schools. The hope is that when local school districts have to pay for unprepared students, the remediation costs will force the local authorities to obtain the necessary funding to insure that students are provided a quality education in the first place. This approach tends to flow from the total quality management (TQM) philosophy of addressing production problems at the source.

In regard to the fourth ISLLC standard, P–12 schools and postsecondary institutions need to establish a more collaborative relationship (Pluviose, 2006). In each state, the P–12 state department of education superintendent and the higher education commissioner need to work in a collaborative manner in order to develop a bond of trust between these two educational leaders and the segments of the educational pipeline that they oversee. We can think of it this way: if the left hand does not know what the right hand is doing, what will be accomplished? From a systems theory perspective, if the parts of a system are not functioning in unison, then the system will not be operating at maximum capability, or in a worst-case scenario, the system will not be operating at all.

Much of the breakdown in the educational pipeline is the result of the lack of communication between the elementary and secondary portion of the pipeline and the higher education segment. All educators in all subjects in each segment of the educational pipeline need to start the process of working together to improve the educational system. Without better communication and collaboration among educational leaders and educators, the disconnection within the educational pipeline will continue.

In regard to the fifth ISLLC standard, educational leaders must always act in an ethical manner and establish policies and procedures that treat all stakeholders in a just manner. Positive outcomes flow from a solid ethical foundation. Fairness and rewards based upon merit provide an incentive to achieve. Favoritism and entitlement have no place in the academic world. Academic achievement must flow from hard work. The academic environment must be free of prejudice and bigotry and focused upon personal accountability and striving for excellence.

In regard to the sixth ISLLC standard, "The lower your family income, the more likely that the combination of family background, community of residence and school and teacher quality will leave you unprepared for college success—whether or not you get a diploma after 12th grade" (Kazis, 2006, p. 13).

The bottom line is that the educational system should not be a depository where students are experimental pawns for various political ideologies and social engineering policies, practices, and programs. The educational system should be about maximizing the learning environment and educational leaders need to be aware of how the cultural, legal, economic, political, and social forces impact the educational process.

Figure 9.1. The downstream portion of the educational pipeline needs to better prepare students for success in the upstream segment.

CRITICAL POINTS TO REMEMBER

- The educational pipeline is abbreviated as P–16 and represents the entire educational process that a student must complete to obtain an undergraduate degree.
- A communication and curriculum gap exists between the elementary and secondary portion of the educational pipeline and higher education.

To further clarify, elementary education generally refers to preschool to grade six (P–6), middle school consists of grades seven and eight, and secondary education (high school) includes grades nine to twelve. Educational research indicates that a gap in the educational pipeline also exists between what occurs in elementary education and the knowledge, skills, and abilities that students need to possess when entering high school; the conclusion is that in grades seven and eight, student performance tends to diminish and leaves students underprepared for high school. Students' lack of preparation then continues throughout high school, leaving them not prepared for higher education. Thus the total disconnection in the educational pipeline can be illustrated as follows:

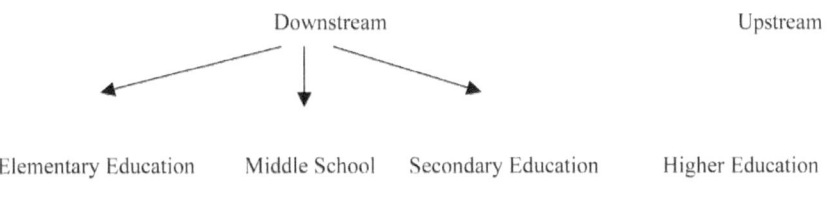

Figure 9.2. The Educational Pipeline

Given the total disconnection in the educational pipeline, no one should be surprised that student performance is subpar.

REFERENCES

Finn, C. Jr. (2006, March 10). Obstacles on the route from high school to college. *Chronicle of Higher Education*, pp. B40–B42. Retrieved September 21, 2006, from EBSCOhost research database.

Haycock, K., Reed, C. B., and Thornton, G. E. (2006, March 10). Student readiness: The challenge for colleges. *Chronicle of Higher Education*, pp. B38–B39. Retrieved September 20, 2006, from EBSCOhost research database.

Hunefeld, R. (2009, November 4). When teachers are the experts: How schools can improve professional development. *Education Week*, pp. 24–25.

Interstate School Leaders Licensure Consortium of the Council of Chief State School Officers. *Candidate Information Bulletin for the School Leaders Licensure Assessment*. Princeton, NJ: Educational Testing Service, 1997. Accessible at http://www.ccsso.org/standards-assessments.html.

Kazis, R. (Winter 2006). Building a pipeline for college access and success [electronic version]. *New England Board of Higher Education* 20(4), 13–15.

Keller, B. (2007, November 7). Teachers seen as making a difference in world's top schools. *Education Week*, p. 8.

Mankiw, G. (2007). *Principles of economics*. Mason, OH: Thomson/South-Western.

Naik, G. (2006, September 29). China's spending for research outpaces the U.S. *Wall Street Journal*, pp. A2, A4.

Pluviose, D. (2006, September 7). Commission's final draft report recommends revamping higher education curricula. *Diverse: Issues in Higher Education*, p. 10. Retrieved September 21, 2006, from EBSCOhost research database.

10

Getting Education Right Isn't Rocket Science, but Many Make It That Way

In a recent survey, 62 percent of district leaders agreed that student performance–based accountability should not be a major factor regarding teacher evaluation (Gallup-Education Week poll, 2014); those district leaders get it, but useless politicians do not. There is a critical difference between accountability and intelligent accountability. As a matter of fact, those who do not comprehend the difference are the ones who also make it extremely difficult to get education on track because they always divert attention away from what really matters in education.

The diverters (primarily useless politicians and educators who have lost their way, are masters at taking something that really is not that complex and turning it into a maze of confusion. To straighten out the maze, we must get back to what education is all about. Simply put, education is strictly about learning. Education is not about solving a whole array of social issues and problems. By diverting education from its primary mission, the task of getting education on track is converted from a straightforward process to rocket science. Quickly an entire industry is built upon an illusion of complexity. Real rocket science is difficult, but illusionary rocket science is like seeing a mirage in the desert; it's all in your mind.

So let's clear away the mirage and get down to the straightforward business of getting education on track. First, I recommend reading *Reality and Education: A New Direction for Educational Policy*, for that book sets the table for understanding the macro realities regarding education.

With that stated, getting education on track begins by understanding the following realities:

- The business or mission of education is only about understanding and promoting learning.
- Learning is defined as acquiring new knowledge, skills, and/or abilities.
- Any proposal to improve the learning environment must flow from the realities associated with education and learning (once again the realities are summarized in *Reality and Education*).
- The educational system can only maximize the learning environment, not student learning.
- Student learning can only be maximized if the student is willing to put forth the time and effort that is required to learn and, secondary to that, if the student lives in a family and cultural situation where education and learning are valued. Ultimately, it is the student's responsibility to learn.

Given these realities, the following obstacles to getting education on track must be overcome:

- There is no room in education for useless politicians trying to impose their political ideology in an educational setting. Paraphrasing Milton Friedman, ignoring the difference between good intentions and actual outcomes is a critical policy-making mistake. Continuing to try to solve societal problems through the educational system is a political folly that diverts attention away from the mission of education.
- The input/output model of business is not the model for education. The inputs in education (primarily the students) are not standardized raw materials that in the end will become a standardized product. The myth or hope of using the business model for education must be cast aside; using an improper model has devastating consequences.
- School cultures that have a negative impact upon teacher performance are characterized by (a) inverse beginner responsibilities, (b) invisibility and isolation, (c) lack of professional dialogue, and (d) restricted choice (Glickman, 1985).

Inverse beginner responsibilities occur when the newest teachers are given the most difficult tasks. Invisibility and isolation occur when teachers are not aware of how their teaching complements, reinforces, or negates the efforts of other teachers. Lack of professional dialogue refers to the shortage of time that teachers have to communicate with each other about academic and professional topics of interest as well as the lack of communication between administration and the teaching staff (Xin and MacMillan, 1999). Restricted choice reflects the situation of teachers facing schedules that are set by administrators and curriculum selection determined by state and federal mandates. This restrictive work environment has been cited as a cause of teacher stress and poor health, which reduces the effectiveness of schools (Kelly and Colquhoun, 2003).

Simply put, for learning to thrive, educational leaders must work collaboratively with teachers to eliminate negative school cultures.

- The teaching of proper values must be taken off the curriculum shelf and once again take center stage throughout the educational system. Values embodied in the Ten Commandments and the Golden Rule coupled with curriculum strategies that encourage the teaching of personal accountability, striving for excellence, and being open-minded to various viewpoints must be re-institutionalized through the educational system. There is no place for moral relativism in schools. Yes, there is a right and wrong, and that reality needs to be communicated to all students.
- The paradigm about competition versus the traditional school model misses the mark; the real issue is equality in funding so that every student receives the same amount of funding regardless of where that student attends school. Equal funding per student opens the door to better educational opportunities for each student. Each school district may not have the same educational program, but each school district will have equal funding per student. Equal funding is the equalizer in education, not competition versus the traditional school model.
- If teachers and students do not have a passion for learning and self-improvement, then the amount of learning will never be maximized. Theory "Y" teachers and students maximize the learning environment. Theory "Y" teachers "never underestimate the power of encouragement" (Reilly, 2000).

- The learning process depends on a commitment to want to learn; many students do not have that commitment and as a result their learning will be minimal at best. This is a fact that must be recognized as part of the educational system. Teachers must strive to encourage learning, and in the end, if an individual does not want to learn, learning is not going to take place.
- Removing Theory "X," or bad, teachers should be a priority; theory "X" teachers do not establish a positive classroom environment in which everyone is respected and encouraged to pursue excellence.
- The myth that the educational system should maximize student learning must be set aside so reality can settle in. The best the educational system can do is to maximize the learning environment.
- The lack of communication and curriculum alignment between elementary, middle school, secondary, and higher education has caused a disconnection in the educational pipeline. P–16 institutions, educational leaders, and educators need to work together to patch the holes in the educational pipeline so learning can be maximized.

By focusing upon the realities and obstacles that impact public education, the educational system can get back on track; we don't need rocket science, we just need common sense. That's the truth regarding education, can you handle it?

CRITICAL POINTS TO REMEMBER FROM THE BOOK

- The current state of public education can be summarized by the following statements:
    1. We've tried just about everything: smaller schools, year-round schools, single-sex classes, after-school mentoring, school uniforms, charter and magnet schools, school-business partnerships, merit pay for teachers, payments to students for performance, private management companies and not-for-profit schools, takeovers by mayors and state departments of education, site-based management, data-based decision making, and just about every idea containing the words "standards" and "accountability." All of these suggested silver bullets promised results, but little has changed (Renzulli, 2008, 30).

2. In the area of turning around troubled schools, we're still lacking the policy and political will to do the job right. We know that at least five thousand of our schools—about 5 percent of the total—are seriously underperforming. Among high schools alone, two thousand are dropout factories. That means that two out of five of their freshmen are not enrolled at the start of their senior year. We know that in thousands of schools serving K–8 children, achievement is low and not improving. If we don't take aggressive action to fix the problems of these schools, we are putting the children in them on track for failure (Duncan, 2009, p. 36).
3. Americans have been at the business of trying to reform dysfunctional schools for decades, with little success (Williams, 2005, p. 237).

- Getting education on track means focusing upon the realities and obstacles that impact the educational system and pushing the other clutter aside. Education is about learning, not being utilized as a system for implementing political ideologies and solving societal problems.
- Ignoring the information in this book will result in an educational system that continues to waste financial resources and underperform. The choice is yours.

REFERENCES

Duncan, A. (June 17, 2009). Start over: Turnarounds should be the first option for low-performing schools. *Education Week*, p. 36.

Friedman, M. (December 7, 1975). Interview with Richard Heffner on *The Open Mind*.

Gallup-Education Week Poll. (2014, June 11). District leaders split on Common Core. *Education Week*, p. 10.

Glickman, C. (1985). The supervisor's challenge: Changing the teacher's work environment. *Educational Leadership* 42, 38–41.

Kelly, P., and Colquhoun, D. (2003). Governing the stressed self: Teacher health and well-being and effective schools. *Discourse Studies in the Cultural Politics of Education* 24, 191–204.

Reilly, M. (2000). *Ice Station*. New York: St. Martin's.

Renzulli, J. (July 16, 2008). Engagement is the answer. *Education Week*, pp. 30–31.

Williams, J. (2005). *Cheating our kids: How politics and greed ruin education.* New York: Palgrave Macmillan.

Xin, M., and MacMillan, R. (1999). Influences of workplace conditions on teachers' job satisfaction. *Journal of Educational Research* 93, 39–48.

www.ingramcontent.com/pod-product-compliance
Lightning Source LLC
Chambersburg PA
CBHW021848220426
43663CB00005B/445